LOVE ACROSS THE COLOR LINE

UNIVERSITY OF

MASSACHUSETTS PRESS

Amherst

# LOVE ACROSS

# THE COLOR LINE

## THE LETTERS OF ALICE HANLEY

## TO CHANNING LEWIS

Edited by Helen Lefkowitz Horowitz

and Kathy Peiss

Copyright © 1996 by
Helen Lefkowitz Horowitz and Kathy Peiss
All rights reserved
Printed in the United States of America
LC 95-49936
ISBN 1-55849-023-X (cloth); 024-8 (pbk.)
Designed by Mary Mendell
Set in Adobe Joanna by Keystone Typesetting, Inc.
Printed and bound by Thomson-Shore, Inc.
Library of Congress Cataloging-in-Publication Data
Love across the color line : the letters of Alice
    Hanley to Channing Lewis / edited by Helen
    Lefkowitz Horowitz and Kathy Peiss.
        p.   cm.
    Includes bibliographical references.
    ISBN 1–55849–023–X (cloth : alk. paper). —
ISBN 1–55849–024–8 (paper : alk. paper)
    1. Love-letters.    2. Hanley, Alice—
Correspondence.    3. White women—Biography.
4. Lewis, Channing—Correspondence.    5. Afro-
American men—Biography.    6. Man-woman
relationships.    7. Massachusetts—Social life and
customs.    I. Horowitz, Helen Lefkowitz.
II. Peiss, Kathy Lee.
HQ801.3.L68    1996
306.7'092'2—dc20                          95-49936
                                            CIP

British Library Cataloguing in Publication data are
available.

To our students
and to the memory of
Armstead Louis Robinson, 1947–1995,
scholar, teacher, and friend

# CONTENTS

# ILLUSTRATIONS

# ACKNOWLEDGMENTS

This has been a collaborative effort from its inception. Without Pamela See's foresight and imagination, the letters would not have been saved or shown to Phoebe Mitchell and historians at Smith College and the University of Massachusetts. The editors and authors are grateful to Pamela See for her careful protection of the letters and for her generosity in allowing them to be printed and photographed for this book.

Smith College and the Graduate Research Council of the University of Massachusetts at Amherst provided funds to support this research. We are indebted to Paul Gaffney of the University of Massachusetts and to Patricia Vidil and Lauren Simonds at Smith College for their careful detective work. We especially appreciate the enthusiasm and persistence with which they tracked down local history sources.

Family members have thoughtfully offered us time, memories, and insights. The late Teressia Hanley's interest in genealogy provided important background information, while Jim Hanley and Betty Hanley generously supplied family photographs.

We are grateful to David Blight and an anonymous reader who offered helpful suggestions for revising the manuscript.

The University of Massachusetts Press understood the potential of this book immediately and offered its support at every stage. We consider ourselves especially fortunate to have worked with editor Clark Dougan, whose counsel and contributions to the volume have improved it immeasurably.

LOVE ACROSS THE COLOR LINE

# INTRODUCTION

Helen Lefkowitz Horowitz

In the spring of 1992, a house is being reconstructed in Northampton, a small city in western Massachusetts. Workers open up a hole in the ceiling. A black lace stocking falls. In it a world lies waiting to be revealed. Stuffed inside the stocking are letters from 1907 and 1908 written by Alice Hanley to her lover, Channing Lewis.

❧

Because the owner of the house understood the potential importance of the letters, she willingly agreed to the request of a friend and reporter to investigate them. From the outset Phoebe Mitchell knew that she had a story. She learned quickly how to find out the essential facts about the author of the letters and the man to whom she wrote. Local Northampton records revealed that Alice Hanley was an unemployed daughter living with her Irish Catholic working-class family. A decade ago, using the reports of middle-class observers and court records, Kathy Peiss had given us a portrait of the "charity girl," a working-class woman who exchanged sexual favors for treats. Had a "charity girl" penned her own words in Alice Hanley's letters in the black lace stocking?

Channing Lewis, the man to whom the letters were written, was a middle-aged man with an estranged wife and daughter living in Springfield, a larger city twenty miles south of Northampton. He was a cook for the aqueduct project that brought water to Springfield from the Little River outside Westfield. It was a dramatic moment when Phoebe Mitchell discovered that Channing Lewis was black. No longer was love across the color line mute: it had a voice.

The love letters of one woman to one man. In the vast sea of American society in the early twentieth century, what can they tell us? Let us consider for a moment the United States of Alice Hanley and Channing Lewis. The census of 1900 recorded that the nation had 84 million persons. A large proportion of them were foreign born or their children. There were over 1.5 million Irish living in the United States in 1900, and more than 3 million persons whose parents came from Ireland. By 1900 the black population in the United States was almost 9 million, 90 percent of whom lived in the South.

The nation was a heterogeneous society. Hardly the melting pot that politicians proclaimed, it was a tossed salad of ethnicities and classes. In this period before World War I, much attention focused on hyphenated Americans and the perceived need for them to accept American values and customs. The society was marked by great cultural differences between groups, but one belief, promoted by the white Protestant middle class, was widely shared, the ideal of the true woman. This standard meshed with the notions of sexual propriety that immigrants brought from their cultures of origin and that black middle-class women, north and south, held dear. Although challenges had been mounted to the notion that the proper female was pure, pious, and domestic, nonetheless many held onto it as an ideal for womankind. Reality had women working in factories, households and laundries, farms, schools, stores, and offices, but ideology linked them to home and hearth.

The cult of the true woman had an underside. If the sheltered woman was pure, what about the woman whose work or interests carried her beyond her doorway? Middle-class women were successful in carrying a mark of superior social status into white-collar occupations, the professions, and reform work. But working-class women in the employ of others found themselves in a more vulnerable position. They were not protected by the presumption of respectability.

In this context, younger women, eager for play and a chance at life, began to shape their own standards of morality at the turn of the century. Working long hours at grueling labor, they earned only half the wage of their male counterparts. Yet they had some income at their command. They could use it to buy fashionable clothes and attract men who could give them an evening on the town. They could exchange sexual favors for treats and gifts. Everyone could have a good time and no one would be the wiser.

Of course, middle-class moral censors were all on the lookout. Every generation of the young has had to face elders ready to deny it pleasures. In the early twentieth century, parents sought to police the boundaries of respectable and unrespectable behavior, and so did churches and charities, newspapers and magazines. But changes were in the wind. Amusement parks, such as Coney Island in New York, attracted crowds and pleased patrons from the working and middle classes. Vaudeville brought popular song and dance to urban audiences. The cabaret drew a more elite clientele as it offered music and entertainment in an erotic mode. Ragtime and jazz were beginning to make their way from New Orleans and Chicago brothels into the mainstream of popular music. Nickelodeons projected flickering images of sensual female beauty. Movies and records were initiating the middle class to this world. Much of the cultural change that was assumed to have taken place in the 1920s was visible in American cities by 1908.[1]

As cities attracted young working people eager or compelled by necessity to live apart from their families, neighborhoods of rooming houses grew up to house them. Entrepreneurs set up saloons, cafeterias, and tea rooms to service their needs. The areas of the city where working-class people lived became known as "bright light" districts and began to attract more venturesome members of the middle class to their amusements. In neighborhoods such as Chicago's Near North Side and New York's Greenwich Village, bohemian artists and radicals moved in to enjoy the cheap rents and lively atmosphere.[2] Although Springfield, Massachusetts, may have been too small to have a full-fledged bright light district, its downtown and Hill areas had apartment tenements for working people, and there were restaurants, bars, and movie theaters.

Alice Hanley, the daughter of Irish Catholic immigrants who had settled in a small conservative New England town, came from an older order that valued respectability. In an immigrant world that saw itself divided between the respectable and the rough, her father had cast his lot with respectable. He worked with his hands but he was, with the help of a patron and his younger children, able to buy a good house in a quiet neighborhood. Alice, as the eldest daughter, was expected to play the role of mother's helper, while her sister and brother added to the family's income. But Alice had other ideas.

She was attracted to men who represented the new. In 1902, when she was in her mid-twenties, she was courted by Mike Manning, a Holyoke bartender. By 1907 Channing Lewis of Springfield had captured her imagination. A black man separated from his wife, Lewis had moved to an apartment on State Street, in the area of Springfield known as the Hill. As Alice took the street railroad from Northampton to Springfield, she crossed from her world into his.

The Springfield of Channing Lewis must have been tantalizing to Alice in its promise of independence. Surrounded not by her family but by Channing's neighbors and friends, she could make a new life for herself. But Channing's Springfield would have been frightening as well. What were the rules? Was she a wife with a responsibility to provide food and cleanly order? Did others see her as a tramp and were they trying to take advantage of her? When Channing was away, whom could she visit? What about Channing Lewis: Did old expectations as well as new promises shape his life? What about the existence in the city of his daughter and estranged wife? What did the neighboring presence of his older, more established brother mean to him?

These letters reveal a couple caught between two worlds. They were breaking the rules of the old order. They were not married; their love crossed the color line. They were attracted to the newer world that promised personal freedom and fulfillment. But they lived surrounded by an older world that valued family, property, and respectability.

And much of the older world inhabited their consciousness as well. This awareness helps us understand a central drama of the letters: Alice Hanley's insistent pleas to Channing Lewis that he make good his promise to give her a suit. All of Alice's aching need to be seen as respectable and as Channing's "wife" became focused on a suit of clothes. In her mind he owed it to her in exchange for what she was doing for him. It was the armor of respectability that allowed her to face the world. It would make her feel good.

❧

Realizing that the letters required extensive research, their owner and Phoebe Mitchell brought them to my attention. It was an exciting moment. As a historian, I turn to history because I love it. History tells a story that satisfies because it is based on real events, structures, and processes. History, however, has one exasperating weakness. At its heart it depends on something out of the control of the historian: sources. Unlike other social scientists, the historian cannot observe the group being studied, administer a questionnaire, or take a survey.

The historian must write from a record that is often maddeningly incomplete. Thus the discovery of a black lace stocking filled with love letters is like finding buried treasure.

I immediately turned to Kathy Peiss and Louis Wilson because both historians have been intrigued by questions that are difficult—perhaps impossible—to answer. What were the lives of ordinary people like? What were the struggles that shaped their lives? As each has bumped up against the hard fact that there were few sources, they have been inventive. When Kathy Peiss decided that she had to learn about working-class young women at the turn of the century and their understanding of leisure, she turned to testimony in court records and to reports about them by social workers. Even if her subjects did not write out their thoughts in letters, others spoke about them, and she could tease out much knowledge from their accounts. To study African Americans in New England, Louis Wilson had to become adept at reading census material and soldiers' pension records. His extensive research on Rhode Island black soldiers in the American Revolution is giving voice to men who have been hidden from recorded history. Both Peiss and Wilson immediately saw that Alice Hanley's letters to Channing Lewis offered a chance for new knowledge about important questions.

For those who practice it, history is a discipline as well as a pleasure. The double meaning of the word *discipline* is useful. History is both a profession with rigorous standards for accuracy and methods of research into sources and it is a craft that requires perseverance and tenacity. Both reporters and historians have to be good detectives. The major differences between their work are the length of time it takes, the level of patience it requires, and the degree of assistance and collaboration available from students and colleagues. Once the letters were turned over to Kathy Peiss and Louis Wilson, the discipline of history began.

The love letters in the stocking were not simple. They proved to be peculiarly difficult to comprehend. It has taken Kathy Peiss and her able graduate assistant several years of research to ground them in their time and place and interpret them. In her essay Peiss helps us understand why Alice Hanley's letters spoke less of love than of longing for clothes and respectability, why they promised food and domestic arts more than the gratification of sexual desire.

And to whom were they written? Here extensive research had to be done to understand Channing Lewis. Because we have no words written in Channing Lewis's hand, not even his signature, his silence has proved more intractable. But much could be learned about his world that would clarify his situation. It is with this goal that Louis Wilson, assisted by tenacious undergraduate researchers, has examined the record left by African Americans in Springfield and in that context has placed what could be gleaned about Channing Lewis.

With this volume the editors and contributors hope that admirers of history—long-time buffs, beginners, and colleagues—will read, question, reread, and understand. The reading as well as the writing of history is a pleasure and a discipline. The pleasure of discovery; the discipline of study, analysis, and interpretation. The book is written for those who enjoy history and those who are just encountering its powers and delights.

This book prints Alice Hanley's letters exactly as they were written and includes a photograph of the original script. The letters should be read with attention, knowing that many of the questions that they raise will be addressed in the essays that follow.

"Unraveling the Mystery of the Letters" not only presents the story of how Alice Hanley's letters were discovered, it also gives readers a beginner's guide to research. Phoebe Mitchell's account is both fascinating in itself and useful to anyone—family member or college student—with letters and documents to explore.

Kathy Peiss's essay, "Love across the Color Line," grounds Alice Hanley's letters in the Irish Catholic corner of Northampton, Massachusetts. Peiss re-creates its dense atmosphere of home, church, and associations and links it to the broader city of workers and middle class, with its mills, shops, markets, and saloons. She offers a sensitive reading of the letters in the light of her broad understanding of working-class women and sexuality in the early twentieth century.

In his essay, Louis Wilson helps us understand "The Springfield of Channing Lewis, a Colored Man." Careful research into the black community of Springfield in the late nineteenth and early twentieth century has not only unearthed the trail left by Channing Lewis and members of his extended family, it has also revealed the network of African American institutions in the city. It has clarified the economic and political position of a black middle-aged breadwinner during the era of segregation.

It is hoped that after coming to the end of the book the reader will return to the letters and read them a second time, with a new comprehension both of a love that crossed the color line and of the psychological and social worlds of Alice Hanley and Channing Lewis.

NOTES

1   For further reading on cultural change see John F. Kasson, *Amusing the Million: Coney Island at the Turn of the Century* (New York: Hill and Wang, 1978); Lewis A. Erenberg, *Steppin' Out: New York Nightlife and the Transformation of American Culture, 1890–1930* (Westport, Conn.: Greenwood, 1981); Kathy Peiss, *Cheap Amusements: Working Women and Leisure in Turn-of-the-Century New York* (Philadelphia: Temple University Press, 1986).

2   Joanne J. Meyerowitz, *Women Adrift: Independent Wage Earners in Chicago, 1880–1930* (Chicago: University of Chicago Press, 1988).

# THE LETTERS

Mr. Channing Lewis.
475 State St.
Springfield.
Mass.

NORTHAMPTON
DEC 9
11-30A
19 07
MASS.

# THE LETTERS

Alice Hanley, Northampton, to Mr. C. Lewis,
475 State Street, Springfield, Massachusetts,
n.d. [postmark 2 August 1907]

Dear Friend:

I will call for my things Sunday evening & if you are not there put them in the hall so I can get them.

Alice.

Alice Hanley, Northampton, to Channing M. Lewis,
475 State Street, Springfield,
22 November 1907

Dear Friend:

I have waited in vain as usual for a few lines from you so decided to write myself. Are you still at the Nelson?[1] I came up on the 8.10 Sunday & found every one in bed so I got breakfast. Papa is sick & John[2] has gone to Boston. I would come

1. The new Nelson Hotel was located in downtown Springfield and adjoined the Nelson Theater; it had a ladies' and gentlemen's cafe, private dining rooms, and "recently opened an up-to-date grill room." *Springfield Directory*, 1908.

2. John T. Hanley, Alice's brother.

down but have nothing to wear. You promised to get my suit for me but I guess you dont mean what you say. I do wish you would go & get it for me & perhaps I wont always be begging. You told me also you know so many people & would see I could meet some of them & get some money so I could get some thing to wear. Perhaps you may think I dont feel it when I cant dress even half decent but indeed I do. Well I wont say any more about it for you know I need my suit but I will never mention it to you again. I will expect a few lines from you or you can call up Miss Ryan[3] 363–2 & she will call me but dont tell her who you are even if she ask. I will know[.] I will now close with love from

Your sincere friend.<br>Alice.

*Alice Hanley, Northampton, to Channing M. Lewis,*
*475 State Street, Springfield, 19 December 1907*
*[postmark 9 December 1907]*

Dear Friend:

Your letter and money rec'd O.K. & glad you sent it for I borrowed my fare from a little boy next door & gave it back as soon as I got it. I can tell you I was pretty sick coming home after waiting so long. Those people were very kind & asked me to wait. They can tell you how we listened for footsteps for hours. The last letter you sent they got it I have not seen it at all. I was too sick to be up & watch for it. And what harm if I was O.K. now but I know I am caught & the Dr. tells me so too. I want to see you & see what I can do. I look like a tramp too but I know in my heart you haven't done right or as you said by me. When you had plenty money you know what you gave

3. Mary A. Ryan, an Irish immigrant, single and middle aged, lived two houses away from Alice Hanley and worked as a "canvasser" (a term often used for a person who solicited business), U.S. Bureau of the Census, *Thirteenth Census of the United States, 1910, Population Schedules,* Northampton, Massachusetts, Enumeration District 695, sheet 3; *Northampton-Easthampton Directory,* 1907.

Northampton, Mass.
Dec. 19. 1907.

Dear Friend,

You letter and money rec'd O.K. & glad you sent it for I borrowed my fare from a little boy next door & gave it back as soon as I got it. I can tell you I was pretty sick coming home after waiting so long. Those people were very kind & asked me to wait. They can tell you how we listened for footsteps for hours. The last letter you sent they got it I have not seen it at all. I was too

---

Alice Hanley to Channing Lewis, 19 December 1907.
The envelope is postmarked 9 December 1907.

sick to be up & watch for it.
And what harm if I was O.K.
now but I know I am caught &
the Dr. tells me so too. I want to
see you & see what I can do. I
look like a tramp too but I
know in my heart you haven't done
right or as you said by me. When
you had plenty money you know
what you gave me. How many times
did I even pay my own fare? but
never mind there is a just God.
& you have a conscience of your own.
You always promised to stand
by me if anything happened +

---

Page 2 of the letter of 19 December 1907.

I guess it has so I hope to God you wont leave one now for I have no one to help me out of it only you for I went with no else. I am all worked up over it. I will be down to morrow if pleasant if not the day after. Dont mite

Your sincere friend.
Alice.

---

Page 3 of the letter

me. How many times did I even pay my own fare? but never mind there is a just God. & you have a conscience of your own. You always promised to stand by me if any thing happened & I guess it has so I hope to God you wont leave me now for I have no one to help me out of it only you for I went with no else. I am all worked up over it. I will be down to morrow if pleasant if not the day after. Dont write.

> Your sincere friend.
> Alice

*Alice Hanley, Northampton, to Channing M. Lewis,*
*24 December 1907*

Dear Friend:

I arrived home O.K. at 9.40. I only had one minute when I got to the depot so it was lucky I caught that car. I forgot to even wish you a "Merry Christmas" but I was exerted. I certainly enjoyed myself for once in my life & never felt sick from it. I am sorry it put you to so much expense. It was really too much under the circumstances but I hope I can do something in return sometime. I expect to go to Springfield to morrow afternoon & if I do I am going to bring you a sample of our turkey & some cranberries & etc.

I hope Mattie wont see you for I am beginning to think I am inclined to be jealous.

Next time I come to stay I will do a little sewing to pass time & we wont blow any more money for a while. I feel really lost when I got home. I am going to try & be down by 3.30 or 4 oclock Xmas so I hope you will be in.

Enclosed please find a sandwich for to night. I will now close with love & kisses from

> Your sincere friend.
> A—

*Alice Hanley, Northampton, to Channing M. Lewis,*
*475 State Street, Springfield, n.d.*
[*postmark 30 March 1908*]

Dear C——

Will you please send me the money for the shoes & gloves you promised me. I am tired of waiting. I am feeling well but was very sick coming home. Lilly goes home Wed. John went to Boston yesterday.[4] Write me at once & will watch for it.

A——

*Alice Hanley, Springfield, to Channing M. Lewis,*
*Mundale, Little River, Massachusetts, 10 April 1908*
[*envelope marked in pencil "Unknown"*]

Dear Chan:

I have just come down & find you are gone. Why didn't you write me you were. I brought you box of nice things but no one to eat them. I found your note & I assure you no one but myself will come in here. I found Tuesday's Union[5] at the door so I knew you were gone. I wont stay only a little while as it is too lonesome not even a clock so I could tell time. Perhaps it is all for the best. I have a very sore eye & need my glasses so bad I left home 10.43 & came here direct from depot. I just cooked myself a piece of ham & will eat it as soon as I write this. I am leaving a piece of bacon & pork 6 eggs & a can of milk in the pantry for you in case you come home you will have something ahead of you to eat. I brought a grand blue fish to broil but will take it over to Aunt Mary[6] as you are not here. & also

4. "John Hanley of the Public market has returned from Boston, wher[e] he has been spending a week": "City Items," *Daily Hampshire Gazette,* 4 April 1908.

5. Springfield daily newspaper.

6. Possibly Mary A. Ryan (no known connection to the canvasser), an Irish immigrant and live-in servant in a house at 345 State Street, nearby Channing's apartment. U.S. Bureau of the Census, *Thirteenth Census of the United States,* 1910, *Population Schedules,* Springfield, Massachusetts, Enumeration District 620, sheet 1.

6 lamb chops, 1 2 more eggs, 2 more slices ham & a steak, as they wouldnt keep. Be sure & write me as soon as you get this & tell me when you went. I hope you will like it & that if every thing goes right you will help me get some clothes. I have always thought you meant what you said so hope it will come true. I need a hat right away. It is Easter a week from Sunday. I will now close with love & kisses from

Your friend<br>A.

Write me at home & tell me all. A.

*Alice Hanley, Northampton, to Channing M. Lewis,*
*care of "Chas. R. Gow,"* [7] *Mundale, 2 2 April 1 908*

Dear Friend:

I just received your letter this morning and you cant imagine how glad I was to hear from you. I had begun to think it was a case of "out of sight out of mind." Many a time I cried since when no letter came. I have only been down once since & I took out three big mice & left every thing as it was.

I have been sewing a little this last week. & house-cleaning a little home. I also raked up the yard. When you send me the money I am going to get a new hat. I have my winter one on yet. Kate[8] has a new Copenhagen blue suit & hat & it makes me feel bad not to look as good as she does for I know it pleases her. When am I going to see you again? Cant you come home some Sat. night soon? I hope so any way for I must see you

7. Charles R. Gow was a Boston-based civil engineer whose firm received one of the contracts to build a filtration system for the city of Springfield; this involved routing water from the Little River Gorge in Mundale, now Westfield. The contract began in early April 1 908 and was completed in December 1 909. Channing Lewis cooked for the engineers and foremen living in the "old Peterson house." *Little River: A Complete History and Pictorial Description of Superior Springfield's Superb New Water System* (Springfield: James F. McPhee, 1 9 1 0); "Progress on New System," *Springfield Republican*, 3 May 1 908.

8. Katharine T. Hanley, Alice's sister.

soon. I will go Sp'f'd some day when I get the money for my hat & will go up to the house & look around. Now Chan I hope you will be true or are there any girls out there? Any "French ones"? I wont say any more until I hear from you but will eagerly watch for your letter. With love & lots of kisses from,

Your dear friend.
Alice.

photo enclosed, in cupid frame.
On back: Channing Lewis, perhaps in AH hand

bill enclosed, 21 January 1908 for Mr. C. M. Lewis, Dr. J. F. Bliss,[9] 75c paid

*Alice Hanley, Springfield, to Channing M. Lewis,*
*Mundale, care of "Chas. R. Gow," 27 April 1908*

Dear Chan:

I rec'd your letter Saturday morning and was glad to hear from you. I came down yesterday and stayed here last night but oh my how lonesome. I read our "Science of Life"[10] until 9.15 & then went to bed. It is now only 6.30 & I just broke some wood & am going to have some coffee before I go. I got the bed & the trimmings all ready I found 2 long brass rods in the pantry & 4 brass balls in the drawer of sideboard. Is that all. Is there any lathes for it. Tell me when you write. I have my hat picked out. It is a Copenhagen blue $8.00. I know you will like it. Wait until I have a suit to match & I will be over to see you as soon as your bed is fixed. I am very anxiously waiting for the time to see you. I guess there will be a grand old time, dont you.

When you were so long without writing to me I was sure you were tired of me & had some new attraction but how glad I am the doubt has left my mind as I think of you night & day.

9. Dr. James F. Bliss was a dentist at the Springfield Dental Association, located near the corner of State and Main Streets in Springfield. *Springfield Directory,* 1906.
10. Pearl Mary Craigie's *The Science of Life* (1904) was a religious and philosophical treatise on modernity and happiness.

You know Chan that a great deal of my happiness depends on you as I know you were always ready to advise me & I think I would never be the same if I had lost your affection. I suppose you will say I am selfish, well perhaps I am.

I opened all the windows a while yesterday & aired the house & washed all the lamp chimneys & dusted. Be sure & write as soon as you get this & write me a long letter as I do enjoy them so. I will now close with oceans of love & a thousand kisses from

Your sincere friend.<br>Alice

1 5 Bright Ave.

P.S. I am going home on the 9.1 o. A

*Alice Hanley, Springfield, to Channing M. Lewis,*
*Mundale, care of "Chas. Gow," 29 April 1908*

Dear Chan:

Just a line to let you know how I am. I have just got my washing out & it looks nice and white. I washed the spread also the shams & bureau cover in our room so I am going to fix it up nice. I dont feel very well as I am sick you know what I mean & was sick only a week ago. Too much shaking up I guess so I didn't go down to the store. I am going to dress now & go down & pay on my suit & will go in & work to morrow & Sat. I am going to send them word. What time did you arrive in Mundale? I shall be looking forward to the time when I will see the place.

My mind feels easier now as I know you will forgive & forget what I have ~~Once in a manger lowly~~ [written in larger hand] done & assure you it will never happen again. I cant tell you how bad I feel about it but hereafter will do the right thing & then either of us wont have to worry. I will expect a letter up home Sat. night from you & I will write you Sunday again. Did you get a comb & brush if not dont for I will bring you one

when I come out there which I hope will be a week from
Saturday. Be sure & write now. I will close with love & hope
you will forget the past. Wait until you see the place next time
you come.

> Your sincere friend.
> Alice

Kisses + + + + + + +.
1 5 Bright Ave.
Excuse paper as this is all is in the house

*Alice Hanley, Northampton, to Channing M. Lewis,*
*Mundale, care of "Chas. Gow," 4 May 1908*

Dear Chan:

Here is the letter I promised to write you but you did not
write me Friday as you said or at least I did not get it yet. I
came home on the 2.30 the day you left. I waited until the
clothes were dry & brought them in & folded them. I brought
the shams & the bureau cover home with me to iron them. I
was sick in bed all day Friday, did not get up at all so I was glad
I was home. I paid $6.00 of the money you gave me on my suit
on my way to the depot. My suit they said will be here by Wed.
& I will have to pay $6 more before I take it.

I am going to help mamma to houseclean & she gave me a
new white skirt & 2 corset covers. & will give me my gloves I
think when I get my suit.

I left my plume to be cleaned. Did you get my letters. I wrote
you when I got through washing, but I was feeling pretty sick
then. You may think I was fooling but you certainly shook me
up awfully. Be sure & write me as soon as you can & tell me if
you can send the money for the suit. I wont say any more for
this time & hope to hear from you by Wed or Thurs.— So will
close with love & kisses from

> Your sincere friend.
> Alice.

*Alice Hanley, Northampton, to Channing M. Lewis,*
*Mundale, care of "Chas. Gow," 6 May 1908*

Dear Chan:

I received your welcome letter and you cant imagine how glad I was when I got it. Your other letter must have been forwarded to Springfield as I did not tell them not to send my mail there until Saturday forenoon & you see it was gone then but when I go down for my suit I will call at the P. Office & get it. I cleaned the parlor yesterday & I served until 10.30 last night. I have my corset covers & skirt made & have started a shirt waist.

You didn't tell me when you think I can come over. You cant imagine how it seems not to be able to go to S'p'f'd and find you there. I suppose I cant come for a week or two on account of getting my suit as the expense is too much but I will try & have patience until the right time comes. I only wish I could be with you always & I would try & be happy. When I go down for my suit I will bring down the shams & go up to the house a while. Be sure and write me a long letter as I will get it myself. You can put the money in the letter. If you can spare the $6.00 send it as that is what I have got to pay. I do not want to impose on your goodness.

I will anxiously await a real long letter from you & tell me all. I will close for now with love & kisses from your.

Sincere friend.
Alice

15 Bright Ave.


*Alice Hanley, Northampton, to Channing M. Lewis,*
*Mundale, care of "Chas. Gow," 6 May 1908*

Dear Chan:

Just a few lines to let you know I received your letter & money O.K. and for which accept my heartfelt thanks. I was down street yesterday & left my frames & had my eyes tested.

They cost $2.75 so when I got your money I knew I could not get my suit so mamma gave me the other .75 & I went down and got the glasses. He said I ought to wear glasses all the time.

I wont go to S'p'f'd until I can get my suit then I will see to your coats also any other thing you want me to see to. It is pouring rain here & it makes it very lonesome. I am going to iron when I get this letter written. Send all my mail home here to me as I will be here all the time. I suppose I will stay in Springfield the night before I go over to see you. What time will I leave Springfield? You didn't tell me if you want a comb & brush.

I have two Henessey cigars for you. John gave them to me. I think I have told you all for this time & will expect a letter Saturday from you so will close with fondest love & kisses from

Your loving friend.<br>Alice

15 Bright Ave.


*Alice Hanley, Northampton, to Channing M. Lewis,*
*Mundale, care of "Chas. Gow," 13 May 1908*

Dear Chan:

I received your letter Monday morning also the one with 2.00 & answered it the very day I got it so I dont see why you hadn't my letter when you wrote the second one. I gave it to the mail man to mail. My suit is there over a week now & I should think you would send me the money if you wanted me to have it. I told you when I wrote my glasses were $2.75 & I got them the day you sent me the $2.00. Drop me a line at once so I can know what to do. With love & best wishes I remain.

Your Sincere friend<br>A.

*Alice Hanley, Northampton, to Channing M. Lewis,*
*Mundale, care of "Chas. Gow," 15 May 1908*

Dear Chan:

I received your letter yesterday but had mailed you one the day before (Wed). I have waited again in vain to day & no letter so I have now decided the trouble lies with you. Here it is going on three weeks since I saw you and you promised so faithfully to send me the money for my suit & you only sent me $2.00. That I put .75 to & got my glasses.

Now Chan I hope you will remember that others may take my place as they have done before but you will never find any one truer than I have been to you. It may be hard to part but if you see fairer faces it is all right. You are not doing the right thing & that you know. There is my suit in Springfield going on two weeks & you wouldn't send me the money only promising. You must have got my letters, as I gave them to the mail man. Will you kindly write me a letter & tell me if you are going to pay for the suit or not.

One of our priests[11] was buried here Monday & after the funeral I brought down your shams & bureau cover & fixed the bed. I was up to the house on the car with Elsie. I only stayed about 15 minutes & fitted on my suit but could not get it.

I wont say any more this time but for Gods sake answer it & dont say you didnt get it. With love & kisses I remain

Your loving friend
Alice

11. Rev. Joseph T. Lynch, age twenty-nine, was assistant pastor at St. Mary's Church in Northampton when he died suddenly on 8 May 1908; he was eulogized as athletic, talented, and zealous. *Daily Hampshire Gazette,* 12 May 1908.

*Alice Hanley, 475 State Street, City [Springfield]*
*to Channing M. Lewis, Mundale, care of "Chas. Gow,"*
*Sunday 11.30 [a.m.; postmark May 17, 1908]*

Dear Chan:

Just a few lines so you will know where I am & how I got home. I arrived in Westfield at 5.50 & left at just 6 oclock arriving in Springfield 6.55. I went over to see about my suit & the fitter was at supper so I went & paid your bill & got my feather & went back & had my suit fitted & it needs a lot of altering. I will have to try it on Tuesday before she will finish it & then it will be sent by express to me. I think it is very pretty & I hope you will like it; then I will be satisfied.

Now Chan some one has been in the house since I was here last Monday[.] The tumbler on the sideboard was on the shelf beside the sink & the matches were down also the can of chicken I left Monday was taken out of the pantry & there was a lamp on the refrigerator & there was none there when I left. You are the only one has a key so if you were here & didn't tell me I think you are mean.

I was not in 15 minutes when Mattie came & stayed about 1 / 2 hour. She told me all about being out home & meeting all your bosses & everything at a dance She was feeling good.

I was so tired last night I could hardly stir so I came up home here & stayed & went to bed. but oh how lonesome I was worse than if I had not seen you at all. I would have so loved to stay but I knew you were uneasy about it so didnt say much. but now Chan I want to come out there one week from Friday for Decoration Day you know & stay well as long as you think best. Cant I stay up where you said.

Now dont put me off for I do so want to stay a while with you. I am going home when it gets dusky. Please do write me a long letter up home as soon as you get this. Dear Chan I cannot live without you so do not be mad at me for outside of mamma you are my dearest friend on earth & the only two I ever look to for anything. Some time when you can spare the money I saw a lovely skirt (white) I want to go with my suit (3.98) but it is grand as it is soiled. I will now close with love & a thousand kisses.

Your lonesome friend.<br>Alice

*Alice Hanley, Northampton, to Channing M. Lewis,*
*Mundale, care of "Chas. Gow," 19 May 1908*

Dear Chan:

I received you very welcome letter & was glad to hear from you. I didn't come home until Monday morning on the 9.10. I went down to catch the 8.15 Sunday night & missed it by 5 minutes so came back to the house again & stayed all night. The front door was bolted & I think who ever came in must have come in the bath room window for the spring was not pushed in so I fixed it or else they opened the back doors. Your coats & vests are there & I missed nothing but the can of chicken. You see the had a light for they left the lamp on the refrigerator & all the oil burned out of it. Do you think it would be Babe?

I dont think I will go down to try my suit until to morrow as I have a dull headache so will go to morrow morning & it will be ready for me to take home by Thursday so I may stay down to morrow night & wait for it so to be sure it fits. Did you get the receipt I sent you.

How are you feeling. You know you had a headache Sat. I hope it is all gone.

I enjoyed my visit only it was too short but then I was so glad to see you even a short time. When you write me tell me when you think I can come over again. I am very anxious to be with you a few days.

I think I have told you all except about my watch. It will be $8.40 all together May 24. Now be sure & write me a nice long letter & if you write to me on Wed. send it to Springfield Gen. Delivery & I will get it Thursday morning as I will go & ask any way. I will be home Thursday evening or as soon as I get my suit. I might as well wait for it as to have to pay Express on it. Be sure now & write me Wed. afternoon. I will close now with love & lots of kisses only I wish they were the real ones from

> Your sincere friend,
> Alice.

*Alice Hanley, Springfield, to Channing M. Lewis, Mundale, care of "Chas. Gow," 21 May 1908*

Dear Friend Chan:

I received your letter this noon & was glad to hear from you but I can assure you my feelings were hurt very deeply by certain remarks you made in it. You ask me who stayed up at the house with me. No one did. Nobody has put their foot over your threshold when I have been there since you were home only Mattie last Saturday night. She came up when she saw the light. You speak of locking up the house & then you wont have to worry you say. I am sorry to say Chan you need not mention the fact to me any more. I will give you the key I have as soon as I see you & will take my things home. I hope I will see you next week either here or I will go out there. I explained to you why I stayed over last night. My suit had to be altered so much I had to try it on yesterday when it was basted & I could not have it until 3 oclock to day & I could not afford to go home & come down again to day or pay express charges on it.

Then you spoke of the hat I had on costing $8.00 as much as if I got it bad. Didn't I always have a nice hat. When I met you first I had a white hat I paid $17.00 for and it was mamma always gave me my hats

Really Chan I am so worked up I have a good mind to end it all & then I wont have to be begging of any one. I dont see as I have any pleasure in life for you always act so suspicious. I am the one has reasons & not you. I appreciate all you have done for me as there is nothing ungrateful about me. You know my coming to your house was as natural for me as being home & I always liked to come & stay when you were there & even now it done me good to go up & stay there a day or two.

I went down to see Lydia a little while last night. I didnt stay long as her fellow (Singleton)[12] was there & George's wife & baby & some other girls. She has gone to Nantucket to day to stay for the summer.

Biasey[13] came up to the back door this morning & said the mail man told him there was a letter left in your box for him so I told him I hadnt the key but would write you about it. I didnt even ask him in. He didnt get any farther than the outside back door for I had it locked. I feel awfully bad to day over your letter & wish it were so I could talk to you & could explain much better.

As long as you feel the way you do about the house I will never stay there again & when I have no key I will not be wanting to go there. I have tried to do right & please you but it is no use. I blacked the stove & cleaned the nickel on it also the tea kettle & washed the wood work all around the sink & the towel rack. I wont weary you with any more foolish talk but will expect a long letter from you Sat. morning. Write me Friday & I will get it Sat. With love & a thousand kisses I remain.

Your heart-broken friend.<br>A——

Write me home (Northampton)

12. James R. Singleton was an African American, born in South Carolina and forty-three years old at this time; a waiter, he worked and lived at The Worthy, a downtown Springfield hotel. *Springfield Directory*, 1909; U.S. Bureau of the Census, *Fourteenth Census of the United States*, 1920, Springfield, Massachusetts, Soundex.
13. Chesley Biasey, an African American born in Virginia in 1874, was a gardener who lived a few streets away from Channing. *Springfield Directory*, 1908; *Springfield House Directory*, 1909; *Fourteenth Census*, 1920, Springfield, Soundex.

*Alice Hanley, Springfield, to Channing M. Lewis,*
*Mundale, care of "Chas. Gow," 4.20 p.m.*
[postmark 21 May 1908]

Dear Chan:

Here is two letters the same day. I am so fidgety I dont know what to do with myself until it gets dark. I dont want to go until then on acc't of dress suit case. I would sweep here but have no broom. We need a new one also some stove polish. I am going to shine the stove when I come down next time.

How I do wish you were here. I would be happy even in the woods with you if I only could see you every week or two. Why cant I even come on the stage in the morning & home in the evening & I would enjoy it. Cant I come out next Thurs. or Fri. or any day even for the day. I wont bother you if I cant help you. I know I am a tease. It will only cost .20 from Northampton to Sp'f'd & 5 cts down in morning & .20 to Westfield & .25 on stage. That will be .60 one way or $1.20 for round fare. I will have my suit to wear & my hat.

I told Davidson[14] about my watch & he said there would be $8.40 the 29th of May.

The interest will have to be paid any way by that time which is $2.40.

You can have ticket when you wish but really I am ashamed to speak of so much at once but dont be mad for there is a day coming when I can repay you I hope.

Now Chan dear tell me who you think was in the house. If it was you tell me & dont worry me.

I wont say any more this time but hope to see you the last of the week even for a day & I hope the day will come when we can always be together. I will close with love & kisses from

Your loving girl.
Alice.

P.S.— Write me a long letter.

14. H. J. Davison's Sons, downtown Springfield jeweler and pawnbroker, advertised "money to loan on watches and diamonds." *Springfield Directory,* 1907.

*Alice Hanley, Northampton, to Channing M. Lewis,*
*Mundale, care of "Chas. Gow," 25 May 1908*

Dear Friend Chan:

Your two letters & postal received also the money. I will get the things when I go down. I put up the curtain in the bath room. I was over to see Mary Spencer[15] when I was down. I have my suit & like it real well but I have no gloves yet so cant wear it. They told me get them from the <u>guy</u> so I told them I could. I will have to pay $2.00 for them so if you can spare it when you write I would like to get them. As for more glasses I cant wear them. I have no nose for them & my own glasses cost $9.50 so it would be foolish to throw the money away for them when other things are needed. I haven't any white skirt that is decent but they will do a while. I dont feel very good to day but I suppose we all have a poor spell. I hope you wont be mad when I didnt write yesterday but it is only one days difference. When are you going to camp?

I will have to sweep down there as soon as I get the broom. It is dusty. I washed the oil-cloth Thursday. Tell me when you write this time are you coming home or can I go out there Sat. morning. I will close for this time as I want to catch the mail man & give him this letter. With lots of love & kisses I remain.

Your loving friend.
A.

*Alice Hanley, Northampton, to Channing M. Lewis,*
*Mundale, care of "Chas. Gow," 25 May 1908*

Dear Friend Chan:

I wrote you a letter this noon but I was in a hurry to give it to the mail man so I forgot to tell you papa is not in Brighton.

---

15. Probably Miss Mary E. Spencer, boarding at 187 High Street, two short blocks from Channing's apartment; no occupation listed. *Springfield Directory*, for the years from 1908 to 1910.

He works in Newton but I dont want you mention my name to any of them people out there because you know how easy news travels. I have lots of things to talk about when we meet. What did you think of Biasey? Do you suppose the mail man would leave a letter in your box? He said it was from an insurance company but I thought perhaps it was a bluff so I didn't let him in at all. Of course I may be wrong but we will talk it over when I see you.

Now this is two letters I am sending you to day as I owe them to you so will expect one Wed. morning from you. Post it to morrow.

I think you are going to like my suit also my hat as it is quite large & I think it is very stylish.

I will say good-bye for now until I hear from you & will write you Wed. again. I hope you are enjoying the country for I thought it was grand. Good-bye with love & kisses from,

Your sincere friend.

A—

*Alice Hanley, Springfield, to Channing M. Lewis, Mundale, care of "Chas. Gow," 1 June 1908*

Dearest Chan:

It is now just ten oclock & I have landed in the old home but oh how lonesome I do feel. Hubbard[16] was not in so I saw Campbell or what ever the cooks name is there. All he wanted of you was to find out what the trouble was with Hubbard or if you thought it would be safe to move his family from Hol-yoke[.] He asked me if I was Mrs. L & I told him yes & he said he guess he met me once before so I laughed to myself. I went down to see Louis & he is going out to see you either Monday

---

16. Clarence E. Hubbard was proprietor of "Hubbard's Purity" bakery and cafe, located in the center of Westfield. It offered meals for twenty-five cents, as well as a dairy lunch, soda fountain, and ice cream parlor. *Westfield Directory*, 1908. See also Hanley's letter of 20 July 1908.

or Tues. morning & he says he has a man for you & that you know him but he wouldnt tell me his name.

I am going to stay here to night & would give the whole world if you were with me. I never got to Westfield until 10 min. of 7. I really thought I would die in the old cart & he was full as he could be. He drove into the Convesary just below you & he gave me a dish of ice-cream (he had it in the cart) & went in & I thought he would never come out. I could see your place & if ever I did feel bad it was on that old cart.

Oh Chan if I could only have stayed with you I would be so happy. If you only knew what your kindness means to me & how the least word hurts me you would never scold me. I know I often deserved it but I do mean to be so good & when I dont there is no one it hurts more than myself. I hope you didnt drink anything for it would be wrong & I do hope we will soon be together never to part until death & then after this wicked life I hope we will be together in heaven where there are no partings. I must be with you or I could not live. Dont think I am bluffing for once I love it is forever. If you can come home Saturday night & I will be down & have some thing ready for us to eat & enjoy ourselves. You have been so good to me I can never forget it. When I hear you say "dear" & "sweet" you dont know what a feeling I have. It seems so good to be dear to some one. Perhaps some day you wont have to work like you are now. We may be the proprietors of something ourself some day. & that is my wish.

If you knew what a different feeling I have when I am dressed like every one else. Really my heart raises & to night I was proud as a peacock going into Mary's & Louis & they told me I would have to treat on the new suit so I gave Louis the 15 cts for a pitcher of ale & I had a glass & came right home. I didnt want them think I was too cheap. Mary said "My but your man keeps you dressed slick.["] Charlie was there & he said Yes her man is O.K.. I was too late to get an order for the rent but will send it in the morning & will send you the money. order receipt.

Try and come home Sat. if you can. Write me as soon as you can for I long for the letter. With oceans of love & kisses I remain

> Your devoted
> Alice.

P.S.. Give my regards to Mr. Daley, & tell him I appreciated his kindness to the fullest extent.

*Alice Hanley, Springfield, to Channing M. Lewis, Mundale, care of "Chas. Gow," 2 June 1908*

Dear Chan:

I have just got through working so I thought I would write you a few lines. I went down street at 8 oclock & got some shelf paper & 6 more packages of seed & a fancy roll of crepon paper for the shelf over the sink & came right back & went to work. I cleaned the pantry & washed the window inside & outside. The paper on the shelves is now yellow & white & I got 2 gallons of oil & filled all the lamps & washed the chimneys also filled the oil stove so it will be ready when you come. I also bought a broom & a wire soap basket (.10) to hang over the sink. I cleaned up as good as I could & swept the kitchen good. I have my seed & the ones you gave me all planted so we can have flowers this summer. Try & come Sat. night if you can. When I went to write I had no paper so made this do. I sent Gunns[17] money too day. I am going home to night but I wanted to clean a little so it would look nice when you come home. I know you are very lonesome out there & only wish I could be with you & help you. I think we will be soon together forever. Something seems to be foreshown to me about it. Perhaps after a while you could get a job some place where I

17. Elisha Gunn owned "Gunn's Block," 473–475 State Street, from 1900 until 1922 and was Channing Lewis's landlord. *Springfield Directory*, 1908; Springfield City Clerk's Office, Registry of Deeds.

could help you out even for my board & a little to help get things & we could be together all the time. I know if you only got a good place where you were suited I would be all right.

Really Chan I am unhappy when I am away from you. I do love to see mamma & know she is all right but aside from that I have no desire to be any place only with you. I could live any place only to have you be kind to me. I know I am nervous at times but I know you wont mind me for I cant help it. I hope you will write me a long letter when you get this for I think you will get the one I posted this morning with it as I could not get it in so you could get it to day but was sorry I could not. Be sure & tell me all the news when you write & tell them you are coming home Sat. How I will long for the day to see you again. Excuse paper for I had no other. If you want me do anything just drop a line. From your devoted & intended

Alice.

Love & kisses a thousand times


*Alice Hanley, Springfield, to Channing M. Lewis,*
*Mundale, care of "Chas. Gow," 3 June 1908*

Dearest Chan:

I am in an awful fix over the money you gave me for the rent. & I want you come home to-morrow (Thursday) without fail & I will wait here for you. I worked here all day yesterday & last night went down to Louis again to see if he had seen the man about working for you & he snapped the money out of my hand & wouldn't give it back so I came home & I have been sitting down there all day to day & running around the streets looking for him to get the money & here it is now 7 oclock & I can not find him or get the money. Little did I think he was such a rogue so you come at once & compel him to give it up. I am nearly crazy over it. He is not working any place so come at once & see what you can do. Mary says he is crazy & begged of him to give me the money but no use. Now

Chan dont blame me for I could not help it only you come & if he dont give it I will have him arrested. I am no fool for him. Come as quick as you can. Love & kisses from

Your heartbroken wife.
Alice.

*Alice Hanley, Northampton, to Channing M. Lewis,*
*475 State Street, Springfield, 28 June 1908*

Dear Chan:

Just a line to let you know I arrived home safe. I met a friend from Hatfield & was up with him & he came up to the house & sat on the piazza about 20 minutes until his car came.

I can tell you it is very lonesome here. I am all alone Kate has gone out since she got up & I am alone & have lots of time to think, think all the while.

I dont feel very well & to think just when sickness did come with all other troubles it is hard to think that is the time you have no one to turn to for help or even a dollar. I know you have been good but I am afraid Chan you finished me that night you hit me. It is too bad it happened so but I will bear it all. Too well I realize how you feel toward me when you never offered me the key, as you did always but of course it is your house & I suppose you got tired of me coming so much.

Take good care of my plants & if you get tired of them or go away give them to no one but me.

I wont say any more this time & if I were to die I am never going to beg of any one. Be sure & write me as soon as you get this if only a few lines for I want to hear from you any way. With love & kisses I remain.

Your sincere friend until death.
Alice.

*Alice Hanley, Northampton, to Channing M. Lewis,*
*475 State Street, Springfield, n.d.*
*[postcard, postmark 29 June 1908]*

Just rec'd a registered letter. Will write you to night. Hope you are enjoying life. Did you go to Mt. Tom yet. Love

A.

*Alice Hanley, Springfield, to Channing M. Lewis,*
*Westfield, Massachusetts, "Hubbard's Restaraunt,"*
*July 1908 [postmark 20 July 1908]*

Dear Friend Chan:

Just a few lines to let you know how I am. Well I feel pretty good only for the one thing and that is getting worse all the time. I got up at 6.30 and did my washing. I got some washing soda & they look fine. so dont say I cant wash any more. Who do you think was in about 7 but Mary Spencer. She was on her way to work & only stayed about 10 minutes.

I am going to see the Dr. about 2 oclock & I do hope he will help me. It is awful to be the way I am & no one cares & the only one in the world I am asking help from is you. I got some ice for even a cold drink is good. Be sure & come home to morrow night for you know if I am cranky I love to see you & oh Chan dont mind me for I know I have got to think so much of you I really think it has worked on my mind. Well I know you dont care to hear this so I wont say any more only be sure & come home. I will make your pillow as soon as I get the pillow at home so you will have some thing to remember me.

Yours lovingly<br/>Alice

*Alice Hanley, Northampton, to Channing M. Lewis,*
*475 State Street, Springfield, 17 August 1908*

Dear Friend:

Just a line to let you know I arrived home 7.30 Sat. night. Kate came Friday night so I was too late.

I am so lame I can hardly stir my arms. I cant wash until to morrow so wont be down for a couple of days. Did the people call for the clothes? If they bring any keep them & I will do them as soon as I come down for I must try & do something. I am almost discouraged & ashamed to be looking to you for every thing. Unless I can see about the watch of course it will be gone. If the interest was paid it would be O.K..

K. was to see pa twice one time he didn't know her or Maggie & the day she came home he seemed quite bright— If you get this to night write me & I will get it to morrow. Hope you are well & enjoying life while the tramp is gone. but never mind I wont always be one I hope & will certainly pay you back if I live & even lose [have?] my health for I know you have been good to be. Love and best wishes until I see you.

Your sincere friend.
Alice.

*Alice Hanley to Channing M. Lewis, Mundale,*
*care of "Chas. Gow," undated [postcard]*

Remember me in friendship,
    "     "  " love
    "     " dear Chan,
When I am far above.

Your wife Alice

Letter fragment, undated
(cf. 27 April 1908 letter)

When you did not write me for so long I surely thought you were getting tired of me & had some new attraction in the way [b]ut how glad I am to think you have removed the doubt from my mind as I think of you night and day. I feel that a great deal of my future happiness in life depends upon you. I [know you] were always ready to counsel & advise me & I think my mind would surely be lost forever if I thought I had lost your intended affection. You may think I am selfish, well perhaps I am.

Undated [list]

| Hat. | | 2.75 | Shape |
|------|------|------|-------|
| | | 2.50 | Wings |
| | $ | 5.25 | |
| | | .50 | Velvet |
| | $ | 5.75 | |
| | | .75 | |
| Total | $ | 6.50 | Hat |
| Suit | | 18.68 | |
| 16.98 | | $25.18 | |
| 1.70 | | | |
| $18.68 | | | |
| Waist | | 2.00 | |
| Corset | | 3.00 | |
| P. Book | | 1.50 | |
| Stockings | | .25 | |
| | | .75 | |
| | | 6.75 | |

Mike Manning, Holyoke, Massachusetts,
to Alice M. Hanley, 15 Libertys Avenue,
25 November 1902

Dear friend Alice

I just receive'd your letter and glad to hear there is no bad feeling existing as I would feel very bad if there was I write this to tell you that I cannot be at liberty the afternoon you mentioned as it is my afternoon on and the man that works for us is out sick. I just got time to go to my meals. I met B. & C. as they were going for the train Sunday Eve, they mentioned the fact that they were going to Northampton I wished them a pleasant time as I believe they did have I almost wished I could go along but you know circumstances alters cases. Knowing their company would be more preferable than mine I decided to go home and go to bed Alice I hope you will not be offended if we do not meet and I assure you if I could meet you we have a pleasant time

Alice trusting this letter will not [?] you hoping we will meet in the near future

I remain
Your friend
M. J. Manning

Mike Manning, Holyoke, to Alice Hanley,
15 Bright Avenue, Northampton, Mass., 1 December 1902

Dear Alice I received your letter and will try and go up Thursday afternoon But I do not know where you live I will leave here about 1 oclock on the street cars. that is the time I get through work I will see you at the at the Depot. I am a little

better from my cold. Charlie told me you were in Holyoke
Saturday night I will close as I am going to a Basket Ball game
Be sure and meet me

From your friend<br>
Mike

Mike Manning, Holyoke, to Alice Hanley,
15 Bright Avenue, Northampton, Mass., 16 December 1902

Dear Alice I received your letter and will tell you last week
my Partner went hunting and come home sick now my Bar
tender is sick so you see I have not much time for pleasure I
was in the place most all day Tuesday if I had seen you I would
give you a hot one something to cheer you up, as it was a very
cold day Alice I can't tell when I will have a chance to go up as
the man that is working for me is under the doctors care I met
Charlie last Sunday and asked if he was going north that night
he told me he had to work the same old story he had to meet a
Drummer. I am just stealing a few minutes to write this
Hoping you will receive lots of Xmas Presents

I remain as ever—<br>
Mike Manning

# UNRAVELING THE MYSTERY
# OF THE LETTERS

Phoebe Rolin Mitchell

*The human heart has hidden treasures,*
*In secret kept, in silence sealed.*
Charlotte Bronte, "Evening Solace," 1846

Renovation work on old houses usually yields little more than piles of dusty plaster and splintered lathe. Knocked down walls occasionally reveal old newspapers stuffed between walls for insulation, or long-hidden architectural details that provide a glimpse into the past life of a house. At times, however, the infrastructure of old houses, the spaces between the walls, below the floors, and above the ceiling, reveals far more. In the spring of 1992, while renovating their house in Northampton, Massachusetts, Pamela See and her husband discovered a hodge-podge of strange relics from the past. They included a crumpled high-button boot, stiff and mildewed with age, old glass beer bottles, a 1940s-era valentine, a catechism book without its cover, and a cardboard can of Watkins Antiseptic Powder.

Among the tattered plaster and lathe that fell from the bedroom ceiling, workers also discovered a small dark bundle. They took it to See, who immediately sat down to investigate. Under the plaster dust, she discovered a packet of letters wrapped in a black lace stocking.

Intrigued, she read through the letters and learned that they had been written by a woman named Alice Hanley who had lived in the house in the early 1900s. The letters spanned a period of a year, from 1907 to 1908, and were written to a Springfield man who, it seemed clear from the letters, was her friend and lover. His name was Channing Lewis. The letters chronicled the details of Alice's daily life—where she went, what she did, and whom she saw. But Alice also wrote very openly about her interior world, what she was thinking and feeling, especially as it related to Channing. The letters, See discovered, revealed a state of mind that vacillated, sometimes quite suddenly, between affection and anger, hope and despair, vanity and servility. Alice might write of her undying love for Channing in one sentence and, in the next, plead with him to send her money for what seemed a never-ending list of clothes she wanted to buy. See's fascination with the letters was further piqued when, in an envelope of a letter dated 22 April 1908, she found a photograph in a small oval frame decorated with cupids. It pictured a young black woman, in glasses, her hands clasped coyly under her chin. On the back of the photograph, in what appeared to be in Alice's hand, was Channing Lewis's name.

I first heard about the letters through one of the carpenters who was doing the renovation work on Pamela See's house. A reporter for the local newspaper, the *Daily Hampshire Gazette*, I recognized the makings of a good story right away and called Pamela, who is an old friend, to ask if she would be willing to let me write an article about the letters. She seemed enthusiastic about the idea, especially as the story might provide an opportunity to learn more about Alice and Channing and what had happened to their romance. We arranged to meet at her house so that I could take a look at the letters and the photograph. Pamela also invited, Pamela Toma, the director of the local historical society, in the hope that she could provide some information about who was living in the house when the letters were written.

The small two-story house where Pamela lives sits at the

*Pamela See with black lace stocking, letters, and
other artifacts, summer* 1992.
Courtesy Daily Hampshire Gazette, file photo.

end of Bright Avenue, a quiet dead-end street in a residential neighborhood a few blocks away from downtown Northampton, a small city in western Massachusetts. Sided with white asbestos shingles, the house is architecturally nondescript, offering few clues about when it was built or the character of the families who have lived there. Like its neighbors, the house has a small lawn, a few trees, and enough parking for one or two cars. Inside, the renovation work that had revealed the letters was still underway. The kitchen was a chaotic scene, with floors and counters covered with various items dislocated by the work. At first glance, I thought that the grimy collection of objects on the dining-room table were Pamela See's household effects that had been displaced in the upheaval. But a closer look revealed that they were, in fact, the collection of objects that had been found in the walls and ceiling during the renovation work. Beside them sat the black lace stocking, still dusted white with ceiling plaster, and a neat stack of grayish-white letters. The envelopes were addressed in Alice's precise, rounded script to Channing M. Lewis at his State Street apartment in Springfield or in care of a "Chas. Gow" in Mundale, Massachusetts. Three others letters, See told me, had also been found in a wall of the bedroom along with the boot and some other articles. These letters had been sent to Alice in 1902 by Michael Manning of Holyoke.

For Pamela See, the package raised several questions right away. How was it that the letters, which Alice Hanley sent to Channing Lewis, ended up back at Bright Avenue? Why had Alice signed two of the letters "your wife" and "your heartbroken wife" when nothing else in the letters suggests that the two were married? And who, she asked, was the young woman in the photograph? With Channing Lewis's name written on the back in what looked like Alice's writing, the photograph certainly seemed to suggest that she had sent him a picture of herself, packaged in what appeared to be the equivalent of a twentieth-century valentine.

When I left See's house, I knew that I already had a good story, the saga of a packet of love letters wrapped in a black lace stocking that was released from its hiding place after eighty-four years. But I also knew that I would write a better story about the letters if I could answer some of the questions that they raised. First of all, could I find out more about Alice and Channing? How old were they? Was Alice, as the photograph suggested, a black woman? Was Channing black, too? If Alice wasn't the woman in the photograph, who was? What was Alice doing at Bright Avenue? Did she live there with her family or was she a boarder or a maid? How was it, as See had asked, that after Alice sent the letters to Channing, they ended up back at Bright Avenue? Why did Channing Lewis split his time between Springfield and Mundale? Where was Mundale, anyway? Did the romance end when the correspondence stopped, as the letters seemed to suggest, or did the two patch it up, get married, and have children?

Like a puzzle without all its pieces, the mystery surrounding the couple's romance begged to be solved. Faced with the task of trying to find out as much as possible about Alice and Channing in as short a time as possible, I turned to the letters themselves for clues. The names and addresses they provided looked like a logical place to start. Pamela Toma suggested several official sources for information that might tell me more about the couple. They included the 1900 census, tax records, marriage, birth, and death statistics on file at City Hall, and city directories, which give residents' addresses and occupations each year. She directed me to the Connecticut Valley Historical Museum in Springfield as the place to go for genealogical records and local history. She also gave me the names of a few scholars who might provide historical background on the lives of those who lived in the area at the turn of the century.

To learn more about the Bright Avenue house and the people who had lived there, I first consulted the well-worn Northampton city directories at the local library. Under the name

Hanley, I found a Miss Alice M. living at 15 Bright Avenue from 1907 to 1912. Living with her were three other Hanleys: James, a coachman and the owner of the house; John T., a clerk; and Miss Katharine, a stenographer. Curiously, no occupation was listed for Alice. I also looked up Channing Lewis's name to see if he might have been born or lived in Northampton, but found no mention of him in any city directory.

While the information from the directories seemed to suggest that Alice shared the Bright Avenue house with members of her family, I needed to determine exactly how they were related. I took my search to City Hall in Northampton where I hoped to find records on the Hanleys. Birth, marriage, and death records from 1880 to 1914 made no mention of Alice at all. None of the Hanleys—related or otherwise—was identified as black. In fact, in the column under "Race" there were very few check marks during the early part of the twentieth century identifying any Northampton residents as anything other than white. I wondered if this meant that there were only a few black people living in the area at that time or—as I suspected—that official information about the city's black population was simply not as well documented.

But I did find some important information. Municipal records for 1912 listed the birth of a son to Mary and John T. Hanley of 15 Bright Avenue. The boy was named John T. Hanley, after his father. I also found records that indicated that an Alice M. R. Hanley had died of enteritis on 1 January 1914 and was buried in the cemetery of the local Catholic church, St. Mary's. She was married to a James F. W. Hanley of 15 Bright Avenue. Was this Alice's mother? I had found no mention of her in the city directory. To try to pin down her relationship with Alice, the letter writer, I checked Alice M. R. Hanley's obituary notice in the *Daily Hampshire Gazette*, past issues of which were recorded on microfiche in the library. The *Gazette* confirmed that an Alice M. Ryan Hanley had died on 1 January 1914, leaving her husband, James, two daughters, Alice and Mrs. David Hoar, and a son, John. Alice had a family.

While I knew it was a long shot, I looked through North-ampton telephone directories to see if any Hanleys still lived in the area. Although a few Hanleys were listed, including one John Jr., none of the people I contacted had any recollection of a great-aunt Alice who lived on Bright Avenue.

I then went to the Northampton Registry of Deeds in the hope that a will might indicate if Alice married or had children. I quickly learned, however, that unless one knows how to find and interpret the information recorded at the registry, the hunt can be hopelessly confusing and may produce information that can do more harm than good. Digging for an hour through the card files, I followed the trail of an Alice Hanley who had left some land she owned on North King Street to her four children. Alice had done quite well for herself, I thought. But eventually I realized that this woman was not my Alice or her mother but a widow, Alice Cahill Hanley, who was also living in Northampton in the early 1900s.

I turned to St. Mary's Church as a more reliable source of information. My guess was that the Hanleys were members of the congregation both because records showed that Alice's mother was buried in St. Mary's cemetery and because Alice mentioned the death of a priest in one of her letters. I was further convinced that the family was Catholic by the cate-chism book which had been found in another wall during the renovation work on Pamela See's house. Happily, the church secretary uncovered several references to Hanleys who had been members of St. Mary's from about 1860 to 1920. As I expected, they included death records for Alice M. Ryan Han-ley (Alice's mother) and James Hanley, who died in 1931. Most interesting, though, was the death record for an Alice Brennan who died in 1920, at age forty-five, and was buried in the same cemetery lot as Alice M. and James Hanley. The information suggested that the romance with Channing ended and that Alice had gone on to marry a man named Brennan. There were no baptismal records indicating that Alice Brennan had any children.

With a fairly clear picture of Alice's family and some clues as to what might have become of her, I turned my attention to Channing. As before, I started my search in the city directories, which were easily accessible, if not as accurate or complete as census records later proved to be. The Springfield city directory confirmed that, from 1907 until 1912, Channing M. Lewis lived at 475 State Street, the address listed on a number of Alice's letters, and was employed as a cook. Records list Channing as the sole occupant of the apartment during this period, although it is clear from Alice's letters that during the year they corresponded she spent a fair amount of time there. On several occasions she stayed overnight in his apartment while Channing was away in Mundale and she tells him in her letters of meeting people they both knew.

Because the last few letters Alice sent Channing in the summer of 1908 suggested that the relationship was unraveling, I half expected the trail to end there. But, in 1912, after Alice disappears from city listings in Northampton, she resurfaces as a resident of State Street in Springfield. She did not reside at Channing's address, but at 453 State Street, close to Channing's old apartment; he had meanwhile relocated to a different residence on Cypress Street. A year later, however, Alice and Channing were living together: both of them were listed as residents at 555 Worthington Street. But the arrangement was short-lived. By 1916, Alice had moved to another address in Springfield, while Channing had stayed put. He remained at the Worthington Street address for another year and then disappeared altogether from directory listings. A year later, Alice's name also disappeared.

Although I now had a good idea of their living arrangements during the time the letters were written and for the eight years following, I still had only the barest facts about Alice and Channing. I did not know their ages. The information that I had found in Northampton City Hall suggested that Alice was white, but I had found no official record that indicated her race. I still did not know if Channing was black or white. To try to find out more about him, I decided to focus my search on Mundale. I couldn't find it on any maps of western Massachusetts. But after another long search at the local library, I finally found it on a 1911 map of the area's electric rail lines in a publication for local businesses. Mundale appeared to be a small town or neighborhood located on the outskirts of Westfield, about fifteen miles west of Springfield. Although Westfield city directories had no record of Channing, they did include a 1908 listing for a contractor by the name of Charles R. Gow, whose name appeared on the letters that Alice sent to Mundale. I also confirmed that "Hubbards," to which Alice refers in her letters, was a Westfield bakery and restaurant.

To learn what I could from census records, I went to the Connecticut Valley Historical Museum in Springfield and met with Joseph Carvalho, its director. I had expected to find the museum a dim and quiet place where only a few older people leafed through dusty volumes. Instead I found the two rooms in which the museum keeps its genealogical and demographic records packed with all sorts and all ages of people, from young men in baseball hats to pregnant women in flower-print dresses.

When I told Carvalho the story about the letters, he was fascinated and eager to assist me in unearthing whatever might be contained in the museum's many historical documents. He spent several hours helping me find my way around the 1900 census and walked with me to the Springfield City Hall nearby where we looked through marriage and probate records. Carvalho is an experienced genealogist who has written a genealogical research book on black people who had lived in Springfield up to the 1850s. He knew how to locate information contained in census records and to interpret what those statistics revealed in human terms.

As I had hoped, the census revealed the details of Alice and her family. It listed five people who were living at 15 Bright Avenue on 4 June 1900: her father, James, forty-five; her mother, Alice M., fifty-four; and their three children, Alice, twenty-four, Katharine, twenty-two, and John, twenty. The records show that Alice's mother had emigrated from Ireland in 1867 and her father, three years later. The children were all born in the United States: Alice in August 1875. That made her thirty-two years old when she wrote the letters to Channing. Under the column headed "Color or Race" each name was followed by a "W": the Hanleys were white.

The 1900 census record held a second surprise: Channing Lewis was black. He had been born in Virginia and had moved to Massachusetts. He was married to a white woman named Josephine who, like Alice's parents, had emigrated from Ireland. The couple had a daughter, also named Josephine, who was eight at the time of the 1900 census. The marriage, which had taken place in Springfield in 1890, was Josephine's first and Channing's second. We found no information about Channing's first marriage.

Carvalho also produced a 1900-era map of Springfield which showed the apartment block where Channing had lived at 475 State Street. Later that day, when I went to look at the building, I found a three-story red-brick building that had several apartments on the top two floors and a corner bar at ground level. All in all, it didn't look like it had changed much from the time Channing lived there.

At the Springfield Registry of Probate, Carvalho helped me locate the will of an Alice Hanley of Westfield, who died on 31 December 1920. Her executor was listed as John T. Hanley. Her personal estate consisted of $339 in debts and about 2½ acres of land in Northampton, valued at $1,000. While the year of her death was the same as the records I obtained at St. Mary's cemetery and Carvalho seemed certain that this must be Alice's will, I had a niggling suspicion that this might be the other Alice—Alice Cahill Hanley—who had led me on the wild goose chase in Northampton's Registry of Deeds. Like Alice Cahill Hanley, this woman had also left her estate to her four children, none of whose names—except for John T.'s—was familiar to me. Given that Alice, by all accounts, was still unmarried and childless as late as 1917, it seemed very unlikely that she had four children by 1920. It was also confusing that the name listed on the will was Alice Hanley and not Alice Brennan, the name of the woman who was buried at St. Mary's in the Hanley lot. By the end of the day spent with Carvalho I knew that Alice was a white working-class woman whose parents had come over from Ireland. I knew Channing Lewis was black and had married twice.

Judging from the tone of Alice's last few letters to Channing, it is possible that the relationship broke off shortly after they were written, with Channing returning the letters to Alice, who tucked them away in the attic at Bright Avenue. Pamela See conjectured that Hanley probably hid them away under the attic floorboards, a space that was accessible because of inch-wide gaps between the boards. "She could have easily lifted up a board and stuck them in there," she explained. Hidden under the floor, the letters would have escaped discovery by the subsequent owners of the house, See said. She added that there is no evidence that any of the owners did any work on the attic or its floor since Hanley put the letters in their hiding place. It was also possible, I thought, that the letters could have slipped through the gaps in the floorboards by accident after Alice stored them in some out-of-the-way place.

When she hid the letters in the attic, Alice must have been convinced that her relationship with Channing was at an end. But the romance resumed at some point and Alice eventually moved to Springfield to live with Channing. The affair seems to have fizzled for good about three years later. Although I now had a fairly clear idea of the course of their relationship during the period the letters were written, there were many questions still unanswered. What had happened to Alice and Channing after they both disappeared from city directory listings? Had Alice married someone named Brennan? Why was there no mention of Channing's daughter, Josephine, who was still alive during the time that the letters were written? Could she have been the person pictured in the photograph?

My story ran in the 1 July 1992 edition of the *Daily Hampshire Gazette*. Pamela See called me a few days later to tell me that she had received phone calls from two people, one who claimed to be related to Alice and another who thought she might be related to Channing. Both had read the story after it had been picked up by a rival newspaper published in Springfield. A few days later, I visited Pamela See's house again, this time to meet with Teressia and James Hanley of Southwick, a town about ten miles southwest of Springfield. The couple had gotten in touch with Pamela because they were certain that James Hanley was the grandson of Alice's brother, John T. Hanley. Along with some Hanley genealogical records, the couple had brought two photographs with them. They included a formal portrait of Alice's entire family taken when she was about eight years old, and a photograph of her father, James, a stern-faced, bearded gentleman.

Teressia Hanley told us that it was a fluke that she had read the item at all, saying that she had only bought the paper that day, a Sunday edition, because she wanted the coupons. But, she said, as she glanced over the article, the name Hanley caught her eye. "As soon as I saw Bright Avenue, I knew that was it," she said. As an amateur genealogist, Teressia Hanley had already spent several years tracking down relatives on both sides of the family, so the couple was familiar with many of the Hanley names I had uncovered in my research. They also confirmed that Alice had eventually married a man named Brennan.

Teressia Hanley said she had gotten the information from one place I didn't look—although I should have: the cemetery at St. Mary's. "I went to the cemetery . . . and there on the stone it said 'Alice Hanley Brennan,' " she said. Family legend had it that the relationship between Alice and her father was strained. One member of the Hanley family remembered a visit to the Bright Avenue house in which she felt an unexplained tension between her aunt and her grandfather. "Her grandfather would just leave the room if Alice was around or vice versa," said Teressia Hanley. "She knew there was something wrong, but just never found out what it was." She speculated that the uneasiness between father and daughter may have been caused by Alice's affair with Channing.

See and I also drove to Springfield one very rainy night to meet with a woman, Carol Ware, who, after reading the article, realized that she might be related to Channing. She recalled an elderly relative, Florence Lewis, who frequently mentioned an Uncle Chan. When she read the article, she told us, the words jumped off the page. "I could just hear Florence Lewis. I could hear her voice," she said. Ware, who is a native of Springfield, said that Florence Lewis was her mother's cousin and was probably born around 1890. "She called him Uncle Chan—I would assume he was her uncle, but not necessarily so," said Ware, adding, "often in black families you have someone you call uncle or aunt or grandma or whatever." (Later research showed that Florence Lewis was the daughter of Edward Lewis, Channing's older brother.) This "aunt," who was considered the family historian, died in the 1950s, taking many of the family secrets with her. Like the Hanleys, Carol Ware said that the discovery of the letters had kindled an interest in finding out more about her family's history. "I can't tell you what I felt when I read this article," she said. "It was like his name was in neon—Channing Lewis, Channing Lewis."

When, in August 1992, I wrote a follow-up story about Teressia and John Hanley and Carol Ware, I was struck by how far reaching an impact the dusty packet had had since it had fallen from Pamela See's ceiling that spring. It had provided a fascinating look at the interior world of a woman living at the turn of the century who was in the midst of an interracial love affair. It had revealed some of the personal history about long-lost relatives for two families. After eight decades of hiding, the letters and the story they told about Alice Hanley and Channing Lewis's romance were destined to see the light of day.

# LOVE ACROSS THE
# COLOR LINE

*Kathy Peiss*

Only a gravestone testifies in public to Alice Hanley's life. Born into an Irish immigrant family, Hanley lived her forty-five years in obscurity. When she died in 1920, she was interred at St. Mary's cemetery in Northampton, Massachusetts, in the plot where her mother already lay buried. Over the years, her father, her siblings, and their spouses would be entombed there. Death returned Alice to her family, but at a cost; the secrets of her life were buried under her married name, Brennan.

Sometime before she died, Alice Hanley wrapped a bundle of letters in a black lace stocking and hid them in the attic of her family house.[1] If cold granite marked her civil role as daughter and wife, the lace stocking summoned Alice's passion as a single woman. The fragile net and fancy design, made by women much like herself, delighted the eye and hand with their elegant refinement and sensuous intimacy. Within the stocking were letters of the heart, dispatched to a lover twenty miles away. Alice Hanley wrote these letters in 1907 and 1908 to Channing Lewis of Springfield, Massachusetts. When their love affair ended, she probably asked Channing to return her correspondence, as was customary. None of his letters survives: Alice either returned or destroyed them to prevent their discovery. Although she married another man in 1916, she had preserved and concealed the memory of her earlier romance.

These love letters register the commonplace. Alice expressed her longing for Channing's kisses, her desire for good clothes, her need for money. She recorded her work cleaning Channing's apartment, her travel on streetcars, her struggles with illness, and, probably, a pregnancy. She described an often stormy, occasionally violent relationship, with Alice tacking from desperation to transcendent happiness and back to despair. It is the social identities of the two lovers that foremost catch our attention: at the time she wrote the letters, Alice Hanley was thirty-two years old, a single woman who lived with her Irish American working-class family and had no regular employment; her lover, Channing Lewis, was an African American man in his early forties, working as a cook and separated from his Irish American wife.

Alice Hanley's letters are a singular record of a consensual relationship between a black working-class man and a white woman. We know very little about such relationships: social segregation, virulent racial prejudice, and family shame made the need to dissemble acute. The very uniqueness of the letters, their specificity and ambiguities, makes it hard to find any sure ground for historical generalization. The aims of this essay are modest: to explore how one woman negotiated "forbidden desires" in the early twentieth century, how she grasped the ethics of sexuality and race as a working-class woman. Yet Hanley's letters challenge us more broadly to understand gender, race, and class not simply as conceptual abstractions, as they are all too often invoked, but as dimensions of lived experience in all its complexity and contradiction.

❋

Records documenting the history of sexuality across the color line are fragmentary at best. For several decades, attention has been focused on the history of racial oppression in the United

States, and it has been difficult to perceive how racism and intimacy might live side by side. Nevertheless, historians and other scholars have begun to shed light on a subject that has been both controversial and suppressed. Their work challenges us to understand these relationships as emerging from specific historical and ideological circumstances. That is, relationships become "interracial" in circumstances where social groups are classified and behave as "races" (based on phenotype or kinship), and these circumstances change over time. Because they are considered taboo, such relationships also powerfully affect the way a society organizes and perceives gender and sexuality in general.[2]

The term "interracial" obscures the precise character of social and sexual relationships that might have existed, not only between Americans of European and African descent, but for those of Asian, Spanish and Latin American, and American Indian backgrounds as well. At the turn of the century, white men's sexual access to black women, once integral to their authority over slaves, continued to be tacitly condoned politically and ideologically. In direct contrast, the pairing of white women and African American men was proscribed. White Americans' justifications for lynching obscured a truth they could not readily entertain, as Ida B. Wells-Barnett astutely observed: their defamation of African American men as uncontrollable and criminal, desiring and raping innocent white women, concealed the fact that a number of black men and white women had entered into consensual relationships.[3]

Concern about interracial sex and marriage intensified in the late nineteenth and early twentieth centuries, manifest particularly in the South and West, but articulated as well in some northern states. This coincided with the reconsolidation of southern white men's control over African Americans after 1877; the rise of scientific racism, particularly as manifested in eugenics; and the growing anxiety over "new" immigrants and urban subcultures, perceived as agents of disorder. Prohibited relationships were embedded in overlapping systems

57

of sexual regulation and racial control. That these systems were under severe strain may be seen in the very visible drama surrounding the black prize-fighter Jack Johnson and his relationships with two white women in 1912 and 1913; Johnson was charged under the Mann Act with criminally transporting a white woman across state lines for sexual purposes. The act had been designed to control "white slavery" and prostitution, yet it is clear that much of what reformers perceived to be sex trafficking was, rather, voluntary encounters and sexual experiments of young women and men.

The Johnson affair brought out with particular force how sexually charged public perceptions of these relationships were, with newspaper reports and legislative hearings offering up a rich brew of desire and denial, fascination and revulsion. The case led to renewed calls for so-called antimiscegenation legislation, even in Massachusetts, which had earlier repealed such laws. The words of a Georgia representative epitomize the viciousness and frenzy unleashed by the Johnson affair: railing against the "slavery of white women to black beasts," he called upon Congress to "uproot and exterminate now this debasing, ultra-demoralizing, un-American and inhuman leprosy."[4]

One of the striking paradoxes of the history of interracial relationships is that a highly elaborated legal and extralegal apparatus emerged to prevent consensual liaisons, particularly marriages, which occurred relatively infrequently in the first place. Marriage rates between Americans of African and European descent were low but they varied by region and locality. In the early twentieth century, only about 1 percent of African Americans in New York and Philadelphia had white spouses. In Boston, however, the figure rose to 10 to 13 percent, with most of the marriages between black men and white women. Relationships between black and white Americans outside of legal marriage, whether heterosexual or homosexual, are extremely difficult to document and impossible to quantify for this historical period.[5]

Although laws and lynching frequently enforced the prohibition on these relationships, undoubtedly most effective in the North were social codes and reflexive understandings forbidding "race mixing." Still, we know relatively little about the place of such informal rules in the daily lives of working people. The public concern swirling around Jack Johnson may have mounted in part because sites for sociability and sexual encounters between black and white Americans had become more visible around the turn of the century. But these encounters had been going on quietly for decades among poor and working-class Americans. The history of Irish Americans' animosity and racism toward African Americans in the nineteenth century is amply documented; less well known is evidence of a small but significant number of intimate relationships between urban Irish and black Americans in the mid-nineteenth century. Servants and laborers, these people were thrown together by poverty, lived side by side, and performed menial work in a job market that discriminated against both groups. Vulnerability and proximity could spark hatred, but it could also beget cooperation and love.[6]

Alice Hanley's letters do not reveal whether her experience was typical or representative, but they do offer a rare inside look at one such romance. Yet here there is an enigma: the letters offer us a firsthand account of an intimate relationship between a white woman and a black man, but they have little explicit to say about racial differences or racial prejudice. Historians are increasingly mindful of what lies unspoken in a text, but silence remains difficult to interpret. Faint traces in the letters point to the discrimination Channing faced in the job market and the conflicts Alice had with her parents; they suggest how the burden of racial difference exacerbated the difficulties they had. But these really are traces: Why was race, in a sense, "unspeakable"? Was it part of the air Alice and Channing breathed, a "metalanguage," as historian Evelyn Brooks Higginbotham calls it, whose grammar needed no acknowledgment yet structured every locution? Was it simply too dangerous, indeed tabooed?[7]

Or perhaps Alice had other things on her mind. She was, after all, poor, unemployed, likely pregnant, and in conflict with her parents. For present-day readers, it is the interracial dimension of Alice and Channing's story that commands our notice and marks these documents as rare and significant sources. But the story is also, less obviously, about other kinds of experiences and differences. Alice was a practicing Catholic, while Channing had ties to the black Baptist church. Alice's "whiteness" was ethnically specific, that is, she was the American-born daughter of Irish immigrants; Channing's African American identity, as a migrant from Virginia in the aftermath of the Civil War, was inflected with a particular regional and generational experience.

Most notably, differences constructed around and through gender and sexuality structured the language in which Alice spoke of her behavior and Channing's. After all, in breaking the taboo against interracial relationships she had also violated the prohibition against nonmarital sexual behavior. Indeed, throughout the letters Alice was most agitated over the ethics and consequences of nonmarital heterosexuality. These were undoubtedly complicated by racial difference, but were not necessarily determined by them.

The letters capture Alice's sensibility and concerns for little more than a year. They are at times maddeningly opaque, referring to people and events now impossible to trace. We only hear Channing Lewis through Alice's voice, and it is difficult to take the full measure of their relationship. There is much we cannot know about the couple, but the letters nonetheless allow us to glimpse a turn-of-the-century world otherwise hidden from view.

❀

Birth certificates, census schedules, and deeds—a handful of official records—disclose a fragmentary picture of Alice Hanley's life before she met Channing Lewis. Her family struggled in the harsh economic and social climate Irish immigrants encountered in the nineteenth century. As Alice grew into adolescence, her family was scrambling out of poverty toward a life of some stability and even comfort. Given the paucity of evidence, it is difficult to know exactly how the rush of feelings she expressed, the psychic pleasures and costs of being with Channing Lewis, were embedded in her experiences as a daughter of the immigrant generation. Yet the family chronicle provides a context that helps explain the historically specific ways Alice Hanley experienced dependency and loneliness, desired refinement and security, and wanted belonging and love.

Alice's father, James Hanley, was about sixteen years of age when he journeyed from Ireland to the United States around 1870. He may have traveled with his older brother John or joined John shortly after landing. According to Hanley family lore, the brothers first sought work in New Haven, but by 1870 or 1871 they had arrived in Pittsfield, Massachusetts, having cast their lot with a young Irish worker, Thomas Ryan, and his relatives. The men worked as laborers on the Hoosac Tunnel, a massive railroad project in the Berkshire hills of western Massachusetts. Initiated before the Civil War, the project to link Boston and upstate New York had cost millions of dollars, employed hundreds of Irish immigrant workers, and consumed many lives. The final push to completion had begun in 1869, just as James Hanley arrived in the United States.[8]

Off the job, James Hanley courted Alice Ryan, whose father, according to a family story, was a contractor on the tunnel project and had hired James. The match may have served both parties well. Alice Ryan was in her mid to late twenties by the time she married; although Irish immigrant women tended to marry later than American-born women, she was older than all those who appeared on the Pittsfield marriage register near her name. James was young—as much as eight years younger than Alice Ryan—uneducated, and poor, and the marriage gave him an extended family and a footing in America only a year or two after his arrival. They married in 1871 and boarded for a few years. In 1873 they moved to 46 Clough Street, on a block that was an enclave of Ryans and Hanleys: Thomas Ryan lived in the house, as had James's brother John before he shipped to Australia, and a "Mrs. Ryan" and a "J. Ryan" lived there as well.[9]

In 1875, James and Alice Ryan Hanley's first child, Alice, was born. Two years later, the family moved to Weston, at the time a largely rural area, not far from Boston. The Hanleys lived with a small group of Irish immigrants working as servants and laborers amidst large landowners and farmers. In Weston, James became a coachman and Alice Ryan Hanley bore two more children, Katharine in 1877 and John in 1880. Little more is known about the family until they moved to Northampton in 1892.[10]

❀

Northampton at the turn of the century was a small city of 18,000, set in the rich farmlands of the Connecticut River Valley. It had gained a reputation as a center of social reform and women's higher education. From the standpoint of its working classes, however, Northampton offered a diverse and vigorous manufacturing base and commercial hub for the surrounding agricultural area. Its entrepreneurs built large factories along the Mill River, and industrial plants sprang up in the outlying villages of Florence and Leeds. Silk cloth, hosiery, brushes, and cutlery dominated the local economy, but there was a wide range of employment opportunities for working women and men. A number of small shops employed skilled workers, while Smith College, the Northampton State Hospital, and other institutions provided many service jobs as well.[11]

Immigrants and their American-born children performed the bulk of the manual labor in Northampton's expanding economy. Building the railroad north from Springfield, Irish

The James Hanley family, ca. 1885. Alice Hanley is seated
between her parents. Courtesy Jim Hanley.

James Hanley, late in life. Courtesy Jim Hanley.

The Hanley family gravestone (front and back),
Northampton, Massachusetts.

*View of Northampton, early 1880s. In foreground, St. Mary's Church and Rectory. Historic Northampton, Northampton, Massachusetts.*

Typing class at Northampton Commercial College,
ca. 1911. Historic Northampton, Northampton, Massachusetts.
G. H. Burnham's Livery and Hack Stables, ca. 1906.
Left, Benjamin N. Moquette; right Henry Cassin. Historic
Northampton, Northampton, Massachusetts

Dewey & Loomis, Groceries and Provisions, 8 Pleasant Street,
Northampton. Historic Northampton, Northampton, Massachusetts.
Bay State Trolley. Historic Northampton,
Northampton, Massachusetts.

laborers had begun to settle in Northampton before the Civil War, clustering around the railroad tracks and mill yards. In the 1870s and 1880s, many Irish immigrants, as well as growing numbers of French Canadians, gained manufacturing jobs.[12] By 1895, as the Hanleys settled into life in Northampton, foreign-born women and men accounted for one-quarter of the city's population: four in ten immigrants were Irish; a growing number of inhabitants were French Canadian; Italians, Poles, Russian Jews, and others were beginning to arrive in small numbers. Most telling, only 40 percent of Northampton's residents had parents who were born in the United States. From the Civil War to 1900, the population of Northampton had doubled, and what had once been a fairly homogeneous Protestant town was now a small city where religious differences, ethnic diversity, and the extremes of wealth and poverty were visible to all. Northampton's citizens could see elements of the social problems endemic to the nation's metropolises, although hardly on the same scale. Tenement houses sprang up among the single-family dwellings. Arrests for drunken and rowdy behavior dominated the annual police report. The school committee wrestled with the problem of educating laboring children and non-Anglophone adults. And the town's established leaders initiated reform efforts to socialize and uplift the immigrant working classes.[13]

Many Yankees held an image of Northampton as a tolerant city, but nativism took hold there as it did throughout the country. One local observer noted pointedly that members of the Congregational church closed their blinds on Sundays to avoid seeing Catholics walking to Mass. Nor were immigrants welcomed into Masonic or other fraternal orders that opened employment and social opportunities for Protestant men. In 1880, nearly all the Irishmen in the town were mill laborers or farm workers and remained cut off from most avenues of occupational mobility during their lives; opportunities widened by the turn of the century, but mainly for the American-born second generation. Fearing that the numbers of immigrants would soon overwhelm the Yankee population, political leaders chartered Northampton as a city in 1883, dividing it into wards that diluted Irish and French Canadian voting strength. Despite these efforts, the first Irish mayor, John B. O'Donnell, was elected in 1891—by three votes in a three-way race.[14]

In this climate, the Catholic parish, composed mainly of foreign-born congregants, sought both to make the church visible and influential and to integrate the immigrants into Northampton's life. Rev. Michael Barry sat on the public school board and chose not to wear the Roman collar about town. At the same time, he built an imposing and strategically placed structure for the parish, St. Mary's of the Assumption— high on the hill near Smith College, overlooking the downtown shopping district, visible to all. When St. Mary's was consecrated in 1885, there were 1,700 church members, the majority of whom were Irish and French Canadian. In these years, Catholic temperance and mutual benefit societies began to spread an institutional web of aid and uplift throughout the immigrant community. In 1891, the church opened a parochial school, St. Michael's, located on a large property called Shady Lawn, which over the years had housed different private schools and institutions.[15]

Unlike many immigrant families that settled in Northampton, the Hanleys did not take up residence near the factories or in the new tenements springing up in the city. Rather, they moved into the rear of a house on parochial school property. The parish priest at the time, John Kenney, was known as a "friend of the poor" and was especially kind to the students at St. Michael's. Perhaps in offering housing to James Hanley he was helping one of the church's needy. It is more likely, however, that the move reflected connections James Hanley had made within and outside the church: as his obituary in 1931 put it, "he had many friends both in Northampton and surrounding towns."[16]

Simply by living on parish property, the Hanleys came into the social and educational orbit of the Catholic church. Although not an officer, James Hanley had close ties to at least one Catholic lay organization. Christopher Adams, a carpenter by trade, had boarded with the Hanley family on St. Michael's property from 1894 to 1896. Adams was also an officer in the local "court" of the Ancient Order of Foresters, a Catholic fraternal and mutual benefit society. The organization, composed of working-class Irishmen—masons, barbers, city workers, bartenders—met twice a month, provided assistance in the event of sickness and death, sponsored social events, and enabled Catholic men to forge useful social and business connections. Within a few years, Adams had become a contractor and builder, successful enough to take out an advertisement in the city directory. Whatever official affiliation James Hanley had with the Foresters, he maintained a close friendship with Adams who, thirty-five years after they had boarded together, was a pallbearer at James's funeral.[17]

Living at St. Michael's also meant that the Hanley children received religious instruction and at least a grammar school education. Although James Hanley and probably his wife could not read or write, they valued learning. Their daughters Alice and "Katie," ages nineteen and seventeen respectively, attended the parochial school in the 1894–95 school year; they were among 113 girls ranging in age from twelve to twenty. The next year, their son John, age sixteen, appeared on the school register. It was unusual for children of immigrants to attend school for so long; the state required attendance only until age fourteen, and most left school for the workplace. Northampton's superintendent of schools complained that immigrant parents were only interested in "the dollars received from their [children's] labor and in the education they can get in a shop or factory."[18]

St. Michael's was not divided into classes at this time, so we cannot know much about the educational attainments of the

Hanley children. Alice probably did not matriculate into high school, which required rigorous diocesan entrance exams and offered only a college-preparation curriculum. More likely, she was an older student at the upper level of grammar school. Judging from the style and content of her letters, Alice Hanley could read fairly advanced texts, but wrote relatively unsophisticated compositions. What is perhaps most striking about her learning is her elegant script and the care she took with handwriting. Penmanship was generally considered a mark of gentility and artistic sensibility in the nineteenth century, and St. Michael's taught the well-known Palmer method of writing.[19]

❖

The Hanleys may have benefited from the religious and social network of resources and support available to working-class immigrants, but they also found a patron among the town's elite. When James arrived in Northampton, he quickly secured a job as coachman to Benjamin Colman Blodgett, known as a member of "Northampton's First Circles." Blodgett had taught music in Pittsfield at the Maplewood Institute, a private school for girls, from 1865 to 1878, when he opened his own school of music. In 1881, he moved the music school to Northampton, where it became affiliated with Smith College. Blodgett's presence was immediately felt in the cultural life of Northampton. He led the orchestra at civic events; he helped found the Home Culture Clubs, an educational and reform organization; he saw his daughter, who was active in local reform for "the advancement of the young women of the city," married to a "son of Old Amherst" in "the most important social event of the season." Befitting his status, Blodgett purchased the Bright estate in 1881, a large piece of property located near the Smith campus. On the grounds were two stables or sheds, which in 1892 became James Hanley's domain for more than a decade.[20]

This was not the first time the two men had met. When he

was a young man laboring on the Hoosac Tunnel, James Hanley had boarded at Benjamin Blodgett's spacious home on Circular Avenue in Pittsfield. James Hanley and Alice Ryan were married not far from Blodgett's house; the priest who officiated was a musician of local note and undoubtedly knew the music professor. No record exists to tell us whether or how Blodgett helped the Hanley family before 1892. We do not know why the Hanleys moved to Weston in 1877 and for whom James worked there as a coachman. Benjamin Blodgett's brother, a wealthy carpet merchant, lived quite nearby, in Newton, but there is no evidence to link the two men. Still, the suspicion lingers that some ongoing tie between Blodgett and Hanley motivated James to move to Northampton. In any event, the two men, whose paths had crossed twenty years earlier, found their lives strangely intertwined.[21]

In Northampton, Benjamin Blodgett became a benefactor of sorts for the Hanleys. He not only provided James with steady employment for about a decade, but he also apparently eased the family's way. Such clientage relationships between working people and their social "betters" may have become increasingly anachronistic in large industrial cities by the late nineteenth century. But even though Northampton grew more diverse and stratified, social relationships still retained a semblance of intimacy and familiarity, especially for those who worked directly for the wealthier families in service jobs. Indeed, despite the social changes that had occurred there, local leaders imagined a place where the qualities of noblesse oblige, patronage, and deference could still be maintained.[22]

In 1897, five years after arriving in Northampton, the Hanleys moved to a house at 15 Bright Avenue, the house where Alice eventually hid her letters to Channing Lewis. Down the hill from Benjamin Blodgett's mansion and stables, this part of the Bright estate had been sold and developed in the late 1880s as a short side street with five houses. James Hanley purchased the house from Minnie Mason, wife of the proprietor of the

Connecticut Valley Kennel. To do so, he took out a $1,400 mortgage from the Northampton Co-operative Bank, a lender that served the working-class population. The two-story frame dwelling, with a shingle roof and "piazza," as Alice grandly called the porch, was modest, but its purchase indicated that the Hanleys had achieved some measure of working-class success and respectability.[23]

Although James Hanley had steady employment, the mortgage payments, more than fifteen dollars a month, may have been too much to bear without the contribution his children made to the family economy. James purchased the house a year after his daughter Katharine, not yet twenty, had found work as a stenographer. John followed Kate into the labor force in 1899, first selling paint and wallpaper, then taking a position as a clerk at Kelton and Company, a "public market" selling fish and meat, in 1902. Estimating wages is a difficult exercise: in Boston in 1907, grocery clerks earned about nine dollars a week, and female stenographers averaged about seven dollars. Even if wages were lower in western Massachusetts, Kate and John together probably earned more money than their father. As was the case in many working-class families, the children's wages, contributed while they boarded at home, enabled the Hanleys to improve their standard of living substantially.[24]

It is significant that the two siblings sought out work in the growing retail and office sector of the economy. John went to the Northampton Commercial College, newly opened in 1896; it had drawn a number of Catholic students from St. Michael's, which offered no vocational training. He suffered from migraine headaches that made it impossible for him to work in an office, and he turned to retail sales.[25]

Kate's position carried the cachet of white-collar work. Two years after she appeared on the roster of St. Michael's School, she had become one of a handful of stenographers in Northampton, skilled work just opening to women. She possibly learned stenography from a tutor or attended the commercial college's earliest classes. Kate's first job, one she held for at least fifteen years, was highly coveted: private stenographer and, later, bookkeeper to banker and manufacturer A. Lyman Williston, working out of his Round Hill mansion. One suspects the hand of Benjamin Blodgett in this. Blodgett and Williston lived nearby, traveled in the same civic and cultural circles, and had worked together establishing the Home Culture Clubs. By recommending a capable stenographer from a reliable family, Blodgett may have done his friend a favor and at the same time, done his coachman another good turn.[26]

Alice Hanley, in contrast to her younger siblings, had no discernible source of regular employment or income in these years.[27] It was not for want of opportunities. In 1895, more than one-quarter of the women living in Northampton worked for wages. Of these, almost all who were foreign born labored as domestic servants or in manufacturing jobs. Many of those born in the United States turned away from domestic work, with more than 50 percent working as factory operatives in the silk mills, hosiery shop, and brush factory. They were mainly daughters of Irish and French Canadian immigrants. Although James Hanley no doubt would have resisted his daughter's becoming a "factory girl," there were other positions available to young women in these years. With her education, she might have become a clerical worker like Katharine. She knew how to sew and might have apprenticed to one of the many dressmakers in Northampton. Some women worked in the boardinghouses catering to Smith students.[28]

Poor health or a physical disability may have kept Alice from wage work: she certainly complained of illnesses and "lameness" in her letters to Channing Lewis. A more likely reason is that Alice's mother wanted her first-born child, her namesake, by her side. Alice never spoke fondly of her father but her love for "mamma" was deep and abiding. In one letter, Alice suggests their close emotional bond by likening her feelings for Channing to her love for her mother: "outside of mamma you are my dearest friend on earth & the only two I ever look to for any thing." She did housework for her mother, who rewarded her with hats, corset covers, and stockings. Her mother apparently cooked on special occasions at Smith College, and Alice helped out: "I cleaned the parlor yesterday & I served until 10.30 last night." Alice knew how to make laundry white, iron drapery and "shams," and grow flowers in the garden. If Kate and John contributed financially to the household's welfare, Alice enhanced through domesticity the "lace-curtain" respectability the family so dearly coveted.[29]

What Alice Hanley actually did and thought as a young woman, before she fell in love with Channing Lewis, remains a mystery.

❧

We do not know how or when Alice Hanley met Channing Lewis. Born in Virginia during the Civil War, Lewis had arrived in western Massachusetts by 1880, following his brother Edward and other relatives in a chain migration begun during Reconstruction. In his early years in Springfield, Channing worked at a paper and cloth factory, married an African American woman, Amelia Peters, and had two children. Tragedy struck the family in 1884 when Amelia died at age twenty-two. Channing married again in 1890, this time to an Irish woman, Josephine Murphy, who had arrived in the United States three years earlier. By now Channing had become a cook, changing restaurant jobs every few years. Although usually based in Springfield, for a period between 1896 and 1898 he lived in Northampton and worked at Daniel and Kellogg's restaurant, bakery, and grocery.[30] Perhaps Alice somehow met Channing in this period, at Daniel and Kellogg's or on the streets of Northampton. More likely, they became involved with each other after 1903, the year Channing and his wife Josephine separated.[31]

Before this time, Alice had cared enough for a Holyoke

saloon keeper, Mike Manning, to preserve three of his letters, written in 1902. In them we catch a glimpse of Alice at twenty-seven, leading an active social life. On several occasions she invited Mike out for the afternoon; she enjoyed a Saturday night in Holyoke with her crowd; she relished company and entertainment. Addressing her as "friend," Manning was a somewhat reluctant beau. He assured Alice that "if I could meet you we [would] have a pleasant time" but, overworked and ill, "I have not much time for pleasure." Alice did not, at this time, object to drinking. When he wrote to explain his absence, Manning observed, "if I had seen you I would give you a hot one something to cheer you up, as it was a very cold day."[32]

Although she was not employed, Alice's social world revolved around markets, saloons, restaurants, and railway depots. She likely shopped for provisions for the family, knew the local groceries and stores well, and, through her brother John, was probably acquainted with clerks, shippers, butchers, and others in his trade. Northampton had a vibrant commercial culture, readily accessible from Alice's house on Bright Avenue. The city boasted a main street known as "Shop Row," with an array of department stores and small retailers, a municipal theater, and, by 1908, a movie house. Although the temperance movement was strong in Northampton, there were a number of saloons and restaurants, some free standing, some located in hotels, where people socialized.[33]

Whatever her duties at home, Alice was not homebound. She traveled frequently on the railroads and streetcars that connected Northampton with the nearby cities of Springfield, Holyoke, and Westfield. The continuous stream of traffic, with people moving about to earn money and to spend it, is one of the most striking aspects of life in the largely rural Connecticut River Valley in this period. The Northampton street railway began operation in 1873 and went electric in 1893. The first run of the day was at 5:00 A.M.; the last, fifteen minutes after

midnight. Streetcars ran daily, including Sundays when pleasure seekers headed to Pequot Park and Mount Tom. Fraternal
orders and large businesses hired special cars for working-class
excursions and picnics; extra trolleys would be put on for civic
celebrations, church dedications, and important funerals. The
trolley's frequent schedule made it easy for Alice to come and
go, and the five-cent fare was her ticket to freedom.[34]

Alice and Channing probably did not encounter each other
in their leisure time, at a music hall, or on an excursion. They
likely met in a working-class milieu where work and leisure
intertwined: the provisioning and sale of food and drink gave
rise to sociability that flowed through the commercial nexus.
These were not places specifically for social contact among
Americans of African and European descent, the "black and
tan" saloons and interracial music halls that could be found
in large cities.[35] In western Massachusetts, Alice's and Channing's paths probably crossed through connections made in
the world of work, by workers on the job.

Irish Americans had established themselves firmly in the
restaurant and saloon trade as owners and as skilled craft workers, for example, as meat cutters and bartenders. The racial
hierarchy of the trade meant that African Americans typically
found work bussing tables and washing dishes, yet the position of cook—which Channing held—could be a fairly prestigious one. In this setting, Irish Americans and African Americans came into contact. Given that these workplaces were also
places of leisure and sociability, their interactions might produce a kind of camaraderie and even friendship.

Alice most likely met Channing Lewis through her brother
John, a grocery clerk and meat cutter, or her sister's fiancé
David Hoar, a bartender. All three men traveled frequently in
their trades or in search of new employment, and they developed a wide range of contacts. John Hanley probably encountered Channing Lewis in the ordinary round of business, selling meat, fish, and other provisions to the restaurant trade. He

knew the African American cook well enough to pay his respects with a present of premium Hennessey cigars—called in one local advertisement "as good a ten cent smoke as can be found."[36]

There is no direct testimony that David Hoar knew Channing Lewis, but circumstantial evidence—the proximity of their jobs—raises that possibility. From 1898 to 1899, when Channing Lewis was a cook at the Haynes House, "centrally located" in downtown Springfield, Hoar tended bar at P. H. Dunbar's saloon and poolroom several blocks away. After a sojourn in Chicago in 1903, Hoar returned to Springfield in 1905, working downtown at the City Hotel, then moved to Northampton to work at the Hampshire House, opposite the railroad station and a short distance from John Hanley's workplace, Kelton's market. City directories do not reveal all of Lewis's places of employment in these years, but for a time he worked at the Springfield depot restaurant. In 1907, Hoar returned to the City Hotel, although he probably visited Northampton frequently to court Kate Hanley. In November 1907, Alice asked if Channing was "still at the Nelson," a theater, hotel, and restaurant complex on Main Street, where, presumably, he was employed. The Nelson was directly across the street from the City Hotel.

Hoar circulated among local political and business leaders as president of the Northampton bartender's union. Lewis also had influential connections, or so, as Alice reminded him, he claimed: "You told me also you know so many people & would see I could meet some of them & get some money. . . ." If David Hoar introduced Channing to Alice, it would probably have been in 1906 or 1907.[37]

❀

In the first extant letter, from August 1907, Alice states tersely, "I will call for my things Sunday evening." The letter indicates her affair with Channing had been ongoing and intimate enough so that Alice would leave her belongings at his apartment, but not so long-lived and committed that Channing had entrusted her with a key: "if you are not there put them in the hall so I can get them."[38] She lived at home in Northampton, but took the streetcar often to see him, stayed overnight on numerous occasions, and at times, wrote almost daily.

This relationship between a black man and white woman was not a secret, but it did require discretion and dissemblance. Alice did not want the affair trumpeted in Northampton and Channing did not visit her there. At one point she instructed him to ring a neighbor, Mary Ryan, a canvasser who had a telephone. "[S]he will call me but don't tell her who you are even if she ask," Alice warned. "I will know[.]"[39]

The racial attitudes of white residents in Northampton were little different from those in other parts of New England, although the local history of abolitionism and reform may have moderated them somewhat. The *Hampshire Gazette's* coverage of race relations generally opposed racial prejudice and supported black citizens' advancement, but apparently drew the line at "close social relations between white and colored." An editorial commented favorably on a meeting of black and white reformers in New York but noted approvingly there was no attempt "to defend or urge intermarriage." At the same time, the *Gazette* reported crimes and scandals involving interracial couples in a salacious and sensational manner. And whatever the local tradition of tolerance, *The Clansman* played at the Academy of Music on its "first New England Tour" in 1909. Northampton's actual population of African Americans was very small in 1900: six-tenths of 1 percent. The city itself, while growing, was intimate enough that Alice and Channing would likely have been seen by family or friends.[40]

Although in Springfield the couple might have met with disapproval from both African American and white residents, their situation was perhaps less charged. Channing lived on the Hill, a neighborhood with a mix of ethnic and racial groups, not far from downtown. Springfield's relatively large black community may have tolerated this interracial relationship if not approved of it. There were other interracial couples and, after all, Channing did have an Irish wife, from whom he was separated. Indeed, his adultery with Alice might have elicited more comment than the fact that she was white. In one instance, Alice even masqueraded as Channing's wife Josephine. She had gone on an errand for Channing to Hubbard's restaurant, where he had once worked, and she spoke to the cook there: "He asked me if I was Mrs. L & I told him yes & he said he guess he met me once before so I laughed to myself." It is also possible that Alice might have been perceived as an African American woman with a very light complexion.[41]

The letters offer only faint clues of the familial opposition Alice faced as she pursued her romance with an African American man. For James Hanley, the affair must have been a bitter pill to swallow: his eldest daughter defied his authority and threatened his respectability, at a moment when James himself had become vulnerable. The fragile security the Hanleys had achieved received a blow in 1903 when Benjamin Blodgett "removed to Seattle" and left James Hanley without a job. In 1905 he mortgaged the Bright Avenue house to his son John and, although he continued to be listed in the Northampton directory, James moved back east to Newton, Massachusetts, where he worked for a widow as a coachman and lived in her boardinghouse. By 1909, as the automobile made his occupation increasingly anachronistic, James became a gardener. Until the mid-1910s, James spent much of his time physically apart from the family, returning mainly for visits. In this period, he seems to have suffered some kind of mental lapse that may have diminished his authority: Alice wrote that Kate went "to see pa twice one time he didn't know her or Maggie & the day she came home he seemed quite bright."[42]

Despite his absences, James Hanley tried to police the boundaries of acceptable sexual behavior and race relations.

When he returned to Northampton, Alice was in some danger. Her father or both parents—her mother's role is unclear—intercepted Channing's letter when she "was too sick to be up & watch for it." On another occasion, she asked Channing to "write me a long letter *as I will get it myself. You can put the money in the letter*" [emphasis added]. When he was away, Alice was fearful that her father would hear about her from one of Channing's many acquaintances. "[P]apa is not in Brighton," she wrote. "He works in Newton but I don't want you [to] mention my name to any of them people out there because you know how easy news travels."[43]

James Hanley's anger and humiliation, barely visible in these private letters, are etched in the public records of property and probate. Several years after Alice and Channing broke off their relationship, James determined to provide homes for his children John and Katharine. After a series of transactions between father and son—taking out loans from each other and transferring deeds back and forth—John finally took permanent possession of the family home in 1919. That same year, James Hanley purchased a nearby property for Katharine and her husband, David Hoar, who together took out a mortgage from James for $1,900.[44] Alice, by then married and "respectable," received nothing from her father.

James's last will and testament similarly declares the split between father and daughter. Written five years after Alice's death, it divided his estate (worth over $7,000 in 1931) between his only living child, John, and his grandchildren, with one notable exception. After her relationship with Channing had ended, Alice married an Irish American man and soon thereafter adopted a son. James Hanley willed this grandson a token amount of five dollars, recognizing his legal existence but refusing to embrace him as a legitimate heir. Perhaps he could not view an adopted child as a "blood" relation, but that belief would likely have mixed with his ongoing fury over Alice's betrayal of the family's honor.[45]

James's frequent absences undoubtedly cleared the way for Alice to see Channing without harm to herself. It is striking that other family members knew about Alice's African American lover and apparently turned a blind eye on Alice's sexual transgressions. Alice's mother cooperated with her husband's efforts to intercept Channing's letters but otherwise indulged Alice. Alice's siblings did not shun her, nor did her aunt Mary, who may even have provided cover for her in Springfield. Alice at times impudently flaunted the affair: on Christmas, a day of religious observance and domestic celebration, Alice took samples of the family's turkey and cranberries to Channing.[46]

❀

Just as her letters screen out paternal opposition to their affair, Alice dodged matters of race when she wrote Channing. She said nothing about Channing being a black man or about her own racial identity. It may be that racial discourses of the time, particularly those that represented black male sexuality, were so powerfully rooted in the imagination that they needed no articulation. Yet a closer look at Alice's letters suggests it was the particulars of her life as a working-class woman that induced her to comprehend Channing as a lover and a man in ways that played down, even obscured, matters of race.

Alice used a language of endearment, not sexual pleasure, when writing to Channing. "When I hear you say 'dear' & 'sweet' you dont know what a feeling I have," she wrote. "It seems so good to be dear to some one." Addressing him as "dear friend," she closed letters conventionally, only once deviating from the formula "with love & lots of kisses" by noting, "only I wish they were the real ones." She described her love for Channing not as a sexual desire but as a transcendent friendship on which she could lean for aid and counsel: "outside of mamma you are my dearest friend on earth." The letters represent the couple's physical intimacy only obliquely, implied in terse comments, "I will call for my things Sunday evening" and "I will be over to see you as soon as your bed is fixed."[47]

At times she wrote of troubles besetting their relationship, but never named their source or content. Her letter of April 29, for example, reveals that Alice had done something grave and harmful. "I cant tell you how bad I feel about it but hereafter will do the right thing and then either of us wont have to worry." What this harm was, however, can only be imagined: a consequence of their sexual relations, a danger brought about by racist attitudes toward the interracial couple? About this, Alice was silent.

On only one occasion might Alice have addressed the interracial dimension of their relationship—when she discovered that she had become pregnant. When she reported her parents' interception of Channing's letters, she wrote: "And what harm if I was O.K. now but I know I am caught & the Dr. tells me so too." In this somewhat ambiguous passage, she suggests that interracial intimacy per se did not cost too high a social and psychological price, except for its possible reproductive consequences.[48] The comment raises a question about her parents' motives for the surveillance: Was the central issue Channing's racial identity? Alice's nonmarital sexuality? Or specifically the visible result of Alice's sexual behavior? Alice, at least, answered the question for herself: No "harm" if Alice was "O.K."; much if she was carrying a mixed-race, "illegitimate" baby.

Anguished, Alice told Channing, "I want to see you & see what I can do." She likely sought an abortion or hoped that Channing would divorce his wife and make her "respectable." If this was a pregnancy, what happened remains unclear. There is no official record in Massachusetts of Alice Hanley bearing a child. It is possible that Alice was attended by a midwife who did not file the paperwork; doctors were expensive and the local hospital did not admit people "suffering the results of a vicious life." More likely, she had an abortion or miscarriage, or the baby was stillborn.[49]

Hanley family lore tells that Alice had a baby who was "so dark everyone thought it was Italian." The comment has the ring of truth: for kin and friends in Alice's circle, sexual relationships between an African American man and an Irish American woman would have been so unimaginable that a "dark" baby could only be safely thought of as "Italian." We do not know when the birth occurred, whether the baby died or was given up for adoption. Still, it seems unlikely that this child resulted from the pregnancy reported in the letters. In the spring of 1908, a suit and dressmaker's fittings preoccupied Alice, an implausible concern if she were pregnant.[50]

Alice's worries about her health were ongoing and became a frame through which she viewed her attachment to and need for Channing. It is difficult to establish what ailed her. She may have been pregnant again in late July 1908: "I am going to see the Dr. about 2 oclock & I do hope he will help me," she wrote. "It is awful to be the way I am & no one cares & the only one in the world I am asking help from is you." She referred often to being "sick," a term used to describe any number of problems, including irregular menstrual periods, pregnancy-related difficulties, venereal disease, or conditions that were unrelated to gynecology at all.[51]

On a few occasions, being "sick" may have denoted the effects of Channing's verbal abuse or physical violence. On April 29 and again on May 4, she wrote about feeling sick— "you know what I mean"—and attributed it to "too much shaking up." In these letters, she chastised herself for causing them "worry," assured Channing "it will never happen again," and implied a dire threat, "[y]ou may think I was fooling but you certainly shook me up awfully." Alice Hanley described a wide range of physical problems, including a "very sore eye" and being "so lame I can hardly stir my arms." Like many Americans at this time, but especially poor women, she felt vulnerable to pregnancy and disease, to her body's disabilities, to her indigence and dependency: "to think just when sickness did come with all other troubles it is hard to think that is the time you have no one to turn to for help or even a dollar."[52]

Yet Alice Hanley was not "all worked up," as she put it, solely out of concern for her physical well-being. The discovery that she was "caught" brought her face to face with the morality of her behavior. If Alice spoke little of her transgression of socially defined racial codes, she repeatedly voiced her apprehension about sexual propriety and ethics. She pressed Channing to honor his commitment to her: "You always promised to stand by me if any thing happened & I guess it has so I hope to God you wont leave me now for I have no one to help me out of it only you for I went with no [one] else." She underscored Channing's obligation in moral and religious terms, observing that "there is a just God. & you have a conscience of your own."[53] Alice feared that Channing would leave her, a theme that runs throughout the letters. He frequently failed to appear when Alice expected him to, largely because of his work, but also, perhaps, because he felt conflicted about the relationship.

While holding Channing responsible for his obligations as a man and as an individual moral agent, Alice pondered her own sexual ethics. To be a "tramp" or to be "decent": these terms defined Alice's moral universe, a universe that encompassed most obviously gender identities, sexual behavior, and economic roles, but must also have resonated with the challenges racial difference brought to her relationship with Channing. Her sexual activity, she sensed acutely, was displayed in her appearance for all to see. In the letter about being "caught," she pointedly observed: "I look like a tramp too."[54]

❖

What social codes of morality and respectability shaped Alice Hanley's sexual ethics? How was female "decency" articulated and reinforced in a small rural city like Northampton? Alice's sibling Katharine offers an instructive counterpoint to the older sister who so violated social and sexual norms. Kate had followed one of the paths of economic mobility open to working-class Irish American women by going into office work. With weekly wages likely above seven dollars in 1908, she had money to spend on fashionable attire, the "new Copenhagen blue suit & hat" Alice so dearly coveted. Kate probably met her fiancé David Hoar at the tavern in the Hampshire House, where he tended bar. They married in 1909 and had a child the next year. Through her white-collar work, marriage, and well-bred appearance, Kate marked herself as a "decent," respectable woman.[55]

Northampton had an unusual way of acknowledging working-class women's virtue, rewarding it with a marriage gift. Smith Charities, established in 1848 to provide apprenticeships to indigent boys and girls and aid to widows, also awarded dowries of fifty dollars to respectable women "in indigent or moderate circumstances" upon marriage, for the purchase of furnishings for their new households. The organization required that applicants "sustain a good moral character" and that their fiancés be men "of sober and industrious habits." "The most popular benefit" of the charity, bridal gifts were awarded to 147 women in 1909, including, according to family legend, Katharine Hanley.[56]

It is tempting indeed to draw a distinct line between the two sisters, respectable Kate and sinful Alice. Certainly American society sharply etched these lines in its scrutiny of working-class women. At the local level, Northampton's press, schools, churches, and reform organizations magnified the divide between sexual virtue and vice, even when their aims were ostensibly focused elsewhere.

In the 1890s, when Alice and Kate were coming of age, wealthy and middle-class citizens of Northampton founded a variety of organizations to inoculate working-class youth against the temptations of public disorder and private immorality. The Young Men's Christian Association and Women's

Christian Temperance Union sought self-control through exercise and abstinence. The White Cross Society, "recognizing the face of the sexual temptation upon every young man," urged men to stay pure, shun indecent language, and show respect for women.[57]

One of the most popular local institutions was the Home Culture Clubs. With its motto "the private home is the public hope," the organization embedded notions of proper sexual and social conduct in its wide range of activities. As devised by novelist and Northampton resident George Washington Cable in 1887, these were initially reading clubs in private dwellings. As the working-class population of Northampton swelled, it turned to settlement-house social work and eventually changed its name to the People's Institute. The organization involved many of the town's business and cultural leaders, including all of the Hanleys' employers in the 1890s.[58]

In the clubs, foreign-born adults learned English, math, and other subjects from Smith College students. Women took a range of classes in domestic science, dressmaking, shorthand, and physical culture. In 1897 a new clubhouse was built to compete with "objectionable dances," commercial amusements, and the attractions of the streets. At Saturday night "receptions," with as many as three hundred in attendance, "drinking, swearing, undue familiarity are not allowed." Hundreds of wage earners in factories, mills, and domestic service took advantage of these programs; two-thirds of the patrons were Catholic, and women greatly outnumbered men.[59]

For employers, fraternal organizations, and parish societies, wholesome recreation was both a symbol of young men and women's respectability and a means of safeguarding it until marriage. The Florence mill owners served up a fare of lectures, concerts, and chaperoned dances to their young factory operatives. The Father Mathew Society offered Catholic men a bowling alley and pool table as wholesome substitutes for the saloon, and opened a separate women's social room as well.

Other Catholic lay organizations sponsored frequent lawn parties, church suppers, and outings: St. Joseph's Society hired special streetcars to take members to Marshall's Grove for a picnic, for instance, and St. Mary's Temperance, Abstinence, and Benevolent Association held a "watch social" one New Year's Eve. Whatever their nominal purposes, all of these activities socialized young men and women into behavior deemed moral and appropriate. According to historian Hasia Diner, despite an increase in mixed-sex activities, Irish Americans were "still committed to both gender boundaries and sexual prudery."[60]

Working-class women in Northampton had a complex relationship to these institutions. We know most about the "Florence girls" who worked in the brush factory and silk mills on the outskirts of Northampton and were akin to young working women throughout the United States. Before 1909, they toiled fifty-six to fifty-eight hours a week and earned on average seven or eight dollars for their labor. At night, said one, "our rooms or homes . . . must be cared for, our washing, ironing, and mending done." They relished the camaraderie of the mills, the pleasure of walking to work together, the "surreptitious lunches and forbidden chats with the girl across the table" when the foreman was not looking.[61]

Some identified strongly with the institutions of respectability, making time for self-improvement and church work. A Florence operative observed that the local "churches, the King's Daughters, and the temperance societies, all number among their best workers girls who, in common parlance, 'earn their own living.' " The working women at the Nonotuck Silk Mill even formed a club to read Shakespeare in their boardinghouse.[62]

Other Florence working women bore the directives and enticements toward "decency" with some skepticism. Many embraced the boisterous public behavior visible among working women in the nation's urban centers. They liked to stay out late at night, flirt with men, and spend money on clothes and a good time. The *Hampshire Gazette* occasionally reported stories of "our reckless young girls." In one account, two Florence women, standing on the brush shop bridge with their escorts late at night, called out to a passing carriage for a ride; the driver turned out to be their pastor, who delivered a sermon the following Sunday on the "night-strolling habit" of young girls. The *Gazette* delineated the popular local image of the Florence girls as clothes crazy and gold digging. "Their meditations have not been revealed," admitted the article, yet proceeded to imagine their musings about "what kind of a hat they should want for winter, or of the one whom they should eventually select to pay for the same."[63]

In their search for pleasure, working-class women apparently even duped the reformers at the Home Culture Clubs who were so intent on providing wholesome recreation. As a letter to the *Gazette* charged, they had discovered that club meetings "make an excellent excuse for the young misses to be away from home in company with boy friends until a late hour." The clubs had unwittingly become places "for meeting associates that they would not dare invite to their homes."[64]

Young working women negotiated standards of public deportment and sexual morality among their peers and families at a time when Americans in general were increasingly concerned and divided about what those standards should be. Popular culture promoted mixed messages about sexual and social mores. For weeks the *Gazette* closely followed the notorious upstate New York sex-and-murder trial upon which Theodore Dreiser based his novel *An American Tragedy*: Chester Gillette had been dating a young woman, Grace Brown, while courting a "society girl"; when Brown became pregnant and pleaded with him to "stand by her in her trouble," Gillette drowned her. The coverage warned upright readers against sexual immorality, but simultaneously offered a titillating tableau of desire, sensuality, and violence to those who scanned the newspaper's pages.[65]

Still, Northampton's residents affirmed and rewarded an

ethics of propriety for "decent" unmarried working women, whereby they would be chaste, earn wages in a factory, home, or shop, and present themselves as virtuous through proper appearance and conduct. Northampton's institutions reinforced the sanctity of marriage and home life through domestic instruction, sermons, wholesome recreation, and bridal dowries. The press celebrated Protestant and Catholic weddings alike with detailed coverage of sumptuous receptions, exquisite bridal gowns, and "beautiful and substantial" gifts.[66]

At first glance, the picture of Katharine Hanley closely resembles the cultural model of the virtuous working woman. But she did not quite fit the image, so firmly fixed in middle-class culture, of the young bride given away by her father to her husband. Kate was already thirty-two, older than most working women who married; David Hoar was Kate's senior by fifteen years and although steadily employed, was a bartender who moved about frequently in his work. Despite church law and custom that marriages be held in the parish of the bride's family, Kate and David were married by a priest in New York City. The reason is a mystery: this might have been a romantic adventure or reflect a degree of parental opposition. For several years after they married, Kate continued to work and live in her family home in Northampton while her husband worked and boarded in Springfield.[67]

Unlike Smith College students or Northampton clubwomen who were secure in their respectability,[68] working-class women felt the question of their decency hovering around them. The margin of virtue between the Hanley sisters might have been little more than an accident of fate. Being born second of three children, having a gift for stenography, getting a good job from the first: this may have been all that was necessary for Kate to make of herself a "decent" woman. Alice Hanley could not apply for a bridal gift because, living in Springfield when she married in 1916, she did not reside in the counties covered by Smith Charities' mandate. We cannot know how she might have presented herself to the philanthropy's trustees as a respectable woman, marrying at the advanced age of forty. Had she lived in Northampton, her sexual reputation would likely have disqualified her.

Being pregnant outside marriage was, according to conventional notions of women's virtue, reason enough for Alice to castigate herself as a "tramp." In her letters, however, she suggests that female decency was not a permanent or inherent condition, but could be achieved, lost, and regained. Promising to reimburse Channing for all he had spent on her, she wrote, "never mind I wont always be one [a tramp] I hope." The term referred specifically in Alice's letters to the prostitute who, selling sex to make a living, represented the bottom reaches of dependency and degradation. Alice was more deeply humiliated by her lack of money than by her sexual behavior. On one occasion she "borrowed [her] fare from a little boy next door," only able to repay him when Channing sent her some money. She felt acute shame over her old and unfashionable clothing, piteously telling Channing, "perhaps you may think I dont feel it when I cant dress even half decent but indeed I do." Disgrace lay in the possibility that she had become and would be seen as a woman without any resources but her body.[69]

Thus Hanley voiced her relationship with Lewis simultaneously in the language of romantic love and in the currency of exchange. Tokens of affection were goods—in both senses of the word—that, in the face of economic and sexual vulnerability, allowed Alice to maintain a fragile sense of dignity in her own eyes and in the eyes of others. Without a job or financial resources of her own, she depended upon a married man for her well-being, but she could not transform dependency into respectability as Channing's legal wife. Whether wheedling money from Channing or demanding it, she simultaneously effaced the sexual-monetary exchange embedded in their relationship. An African American in a discriminatory labor market, Channing himself was vulnerable as a provider.

At various times he lashed out at Alice, calling her a prostitute when she asked for too much. In response Alice held onto a notion of moral economy. "When you had plenty money you know what you gave me," she wrote. "How many times did I even pay my own fare?"[70]

In the face of behavior that defied social custom and religious teachings, Alice sought to render the illicit relationship normal, even sacred. Gift-giving bore the heavy burden of creating the binding covenant that could not be made through marriage.

❀

Alice thought she could achieve the respectability she coveted by clothing herself in it. She craved fashion with a passion seemingly equal to her feelings for Channing Lewis. Significantly, one of the few objects she preserved with her letters to Channing was an itemized list of clothing and accessories. Alice envied her sister Kate's attire, however she disingenuously skirted the issue: "it makes me feel bad not to look as good as she does for I know it pleases her."[71] The felt need to look "decent" and fashionable animated Alice in her relationship with Channing and brought her great joy and sorrow.

Over a number of weeks, the "drama of the suit" consumed Alice. As spring approached, the newspapers were filled with advertisements for the latest "Prince Chap" and "Panama Cutaway" suits, "fashionable large sailors," and smaller "so-called practical hats." She ordered a suit and hat in "Copenhagen blue" (in fashion that season), had an endless series of fittings, fretted over her accessories, and in letter after letter badgered Channing for the payments. The suit cost twelve dollars, a relatively low price in 1908. The more prestigious department stores in Springfield, like Forbes and Wallace, advertised ladies' suits with prices starting at fifteen dollars and rising to sixty. Still the garment must have cost Channing Lewis at least a week's wages.[72]

Advertisement for Easter suits, spring 1908.
Daily Hampshire Gazette, file photo.

Alice ordered the suit from a store in downtown Springfield, where twenty-seven establishments sold "ladies' cloaks and suits." She may have bought it at The Washington, a cheaper shop that advertised Easter suit "specials" ranging from $12.75 to $19.59. Alice often passed by the store, located on the corner of Main and State; Channing went to a dentist in the building; and she bought or pawned a watch from a jeweler-pawnbroker across the street.[73]

Department stores offered fashionable patterns, fabrics, and tailoring but were cheaper than going to a modiste. The dressmakers' trade had begun its decline as ready-to-wear fashions—with their looser styles and lower costs—began to compete for women's dollars. Alice insisted upon a well-tailored suit, returning several times to have it fitted. For women of her generation, "fit" was a subtle but legible sign of affluence and taste that ready-made could not convey. In an 1891 article, Northampton dressmakers stressed the importance of fit. "To my perfect fitting I owe my success and popularity," observed Madam Lloyd. "You cannot make a $5 suit and have it fit," warned Miss L. C. Knapp. "People who know a good fit know that they have to pay for it."[74] Alice was well aware of this principle.

As Easter approached, Alice worried that she still wore her winter hat. The hat was a particularly sensitive index of respectability and style. "Hats of enormous size," their large brims trimmed with ribbons, plumes, and birds' wings, were the rage in 1908. They certainly created quite an impression—and some commotion—in public. "Big hats in church hide the few men," announced one writer in the *Hampshire Gazette*, while another complained about "dodging under and over hat brims" while "travelling in crowded cars." This was precisely the kind of hat Alice coveted: "I think you are going to like . . . my hat as it is quite large & I think it is very stylish."[75]

Alice had a finely honed sense of the semiotics of style. At one point she complained, "I have my suit & like it real well but I have no gloves yet so cant wear it." The well-fitted, tailored suit, embellished with hat, stockings, pocketbook, and watch, conveyed a woman's "decency" and right to social participation, to friends and strangers alike.[76]

When finally dressed in the full ensemble, Alice had a transcendent moment: "If you knew what a different feeling I have when I am dressed like every one else. Really my heart raises & to night I was proud as a peacock going into Mary's & Louis." She reported her friends' comments: "Mary said 'My but your man keeps you dressed slick.['] Charlie was there & he said Yes her man is O.K."[77] The suit bespoke Alice's respectability; ironically she wanted to be "dressed like everyone else," but she knew well that style distinguished her from the poor, from immigrants, from "tramps." The suit also registered Channing's masculine success as a breadwinner, which may have been particularly meaningful given the discrimination African American men faced in the labor market. His willingness—however grudging—to make good on the promised suit also made clear his commitment to her.

Yet Alice's attire was a flash point in their relationship. Ironically, the very clothes she desired for the decency they conveyed focused questions in Channing's mind about Alice's morality. He watched as Alice shopped for a hat, ordered a suit, and bought a timepiece on credit at breakneck speed. In less than a month, she had run up bills totaling more than thirty dollars. With millinery, silks, toiletries, hose, and jewelry beckoning in the shops and advertisements, Alice's needs and wants seemed insatiable: "Some time when you can spare the money I saw a lovely skirt." Was Alice a gold-digger? The thought crossed Channing's mind. For stretches of time he chose not to write or send money to cover the dressmaker's bills and jeweler's payments, despite Alice's entreaties. "I have waited again in vain to day & no letter so I have now decided the trouble lies with you," Alice wrote. "Here it is going on three weeks since I saw you and you promised so faithfully to send me the money for my suit."[78]

In May 1908, when Alice wrote Channing that someone had broken into his apartment and taken a can of chicken, he accused her of unfaithfulness and prostitution while he was away. "You ask me who stayed up at the house with me," Alice wrote. "No one did. . . . Then you spoke of the hat I had on costing $8.00 as much as if I got it bad." Alice defended her honor: "Didn't I always have a nice hat. When I met you first I had a white hat I paid $17.00 for and it was mamma always gave me my hats."[79]

To confirm her own constancy and commitment, Alice plied Channing with small gifts and domestic services, offering him a comb and brush, seeing after his suits, and serving up edibles. One day she mailed a sandwich with her letter for his evening snack. Another time she brought a "box of nice things" containing the makings of a feast to Channing's apartment, only to find him gone. She left "a piece of bacon & pork 6 eggs & a can of milk in the pantry" and took the rest of the largesse—a "grand blue fish," "6 lamb chops, 12 more eggs, 2 more slices ham & a steak" to her aunt's. Given Alice's poverty and the retail price of these items—conservatively, about two dollars—they probably came from her brother John, employed at a meat and fish market.[80]

Most of all, she reported in exacting detail her efforts to make his apartment a home for the two of them. "I have just got my washing out & it looks nice and white," she wrote. "I washed the spread also the shams & bureau cover in our room so I am going to fix it up nice." Alice clearly took pride in her domestic labor and bristled at Channing's criticism of her laundering. Answering his accusations of sexual infidelity, she cataloged her domestic work as proof against the charge, a response she did not perceive as incommensurate with the allegation: "I have tried to do right & please you but it is no use. I blacked the stove & cleaned the nickel on it also the tea kettle & washed the wood work all around the sink & the towel rack."[81] For Alice, domestic labor, not contracted for but freely given, was the purview of and thus metonym for a wife, not a "tramp."

❁

In the 1910 manuscript census schedule, one of the few official records of this relationship, Alice appeared as Channing's "housekeeper." It must have been a painful label for Alice, who wanted above all to call herself Channing's wife, a promise that Channing both held out and withheld. Occasionally she does so, signing herself "your devoted and intended," and one time, "your heartbroken wife."[82] That these words occurred together is no accident: Alice's use of the language of courtship and marriage coincided with a period of intensifying suspicion and recrimination on Channing's part.

In April 1908, when Channing landed a job as cook on a large-scale public works project, the moment filled the two with a new sense of possibility. "Write me at home & tell me all," Alice directed Channing, who had gone out to the camp at Mundale. Channing's sojourn there seems to have raised the stakes in their relationship. In light of his new job and perhaps her pregnancy, Channing appears to have made a deeper level of commitment to Alice. He accepted her routine presence in his apartment and even entrusted her with the key. She increasingly carried out tasks on his behalf, for instance, meeting with a cook at Hubbard's restaurant, and handling the rent payment. She became part of a circle of Channing's neighbors and acquaintances—a mix of African American, Italian, and Irish working men and women—living near the Springfield Armory. Most of all, Alice's thoughts turned toward creating a domestic life with Channing, as she fixed up the apartment with shelf paper, filled oil lamps, and planted seeds "so we can have flowers this summer."[83]

The circumstances of daily life cruelly conspired to betray these hopes. Alice's demands for money and her emotional neediness, Channing's withdrawal and distrust, spiraled in those months of separation. When Channing failed to write, Alice worried over the strength of his commitment. Although the *Springfield Republican* claimed women to be "an unknown quantity in this camp," Alice imagined prostitutes and sexual temptation at Mundale. "Now Chan I hope you will be true or are there any girls out there?" she asked. "Any '*French ones*'?"[84]

Each attempt Alice made to move toward her vision of domestic happiness was thwarted: by the burglary of Channing's apartment, by a neighbor's theft of the rent money, by her claims on Channing's income. She sought every opportunity to visit Channing at the Mundale construction site, but Channing, mindful of the risks to his job, put her off. "I knew you were uneasy about it so didnt say much," she wrote. By mid-June, Channing had left, or lost, his job. In a round of mutual recrimination, Channing called her a "tramp" and questioned her faithfulness, while Alice countered, "I am the one has reasons & not you." When Channing threatened to lock up the house, Alice, hurt and angry, returned the key. The turbulence culminated in an act of violence: "I know you have been good but I am afraid Chan you finished me that night you hit me." At home in Northampton, alone, she had "lots of time to think, think all the while." Did Alice see the irony in her situation, that her Irish father and black lover viewed her in similar ways, sharing a patriarchal anger and wish to govern her sexual and social life? She certainly realized with anguish and bewilderment that what gave her such pleasure—"[y]ou know my coming to your house was as natural for me as being home"— had provoked in him pain and anger. "I suppose you got tired of me coming so much," she reflected. "It is too bad it happened so but I will bear it all."[85]

❖

Alice articulated the practical difficulties and ethical dilemmas of her relationship in religious terms. How regular a participant Alice was in Catholic social and devotional life—whether, for instance, she belonged to a women's sodality or a "women's court" of the Ancient Order of Foresters—is unknown. But she did go to parochial school and apparently attended church. She was one of the throng at the funeral of Rev. Joseph Lynch, a young, athletic, and charismatic priest who died suddenly in May 1908.[86]

Alice also embraced certain religious teachings, including temperance. In Northampton's vigorous temperance movement in the late nineteenth century, such Catholic organizations as the Father Mathew Society and St. Mary's Society, the latter organized in Alice's church, were active and powerful. At one point Alice warned Channing that alcohol was sinful—"I hope you didnt drink anything for it would be wrong"—and impeded their chances to get ahead and be together. Temperance was a moral tenet but it also encapsulated a set of attitudes about bodily well-being and social propriety. Whatever her commitment to the principle, in the same letter Alice yielded to another view of correct behavior, based on the sociability and mutuality of working-class culture. In celebration of her suit, Alice treated her friends to a pitcher of ale because "I didnt want them [to] think I was too cheap."[87]

Alice never explained directly how she reconciled her behavior with Catholic teachings on sexuality. The church hierarchy had little to say in these years about interracial relationships. A "mixed marriage" was, by definition, one between a Catholic and a non-Catholic. These the church opposed, warning of the "almost certain unhappiness awaiting the members of such unions." The church resolutely affirmed the sanctity of marriage and the evil of sexuality outside of it. Alice was not merely living with contradictions, she was living in sin.[88]

Alice's words may offer a few clues. When she laid bare her feelings, Alice often used a language of transcendent love that mimicked the dime novels and romance stories working-class women so avidly read. "I must be with you or I could not live," she wrote. "Dont think I am bluffing for once I love it is forever." And again, "I would be happy even in the woods with you if I only could see you every week or two." Nineteenth-century Irish American culture may have downplayed romantic love, but Alice and her peers had access to a wide range of cultural sources that celebrated it.[89]

At the same time, the repertoire of sentiments that course through Alice's letters had a religious inflection. In a statement at once formulaic and guileless, she imagined an afterlife together with Channing: "never to part until death & then after this wicked life I hope we will be together in heaven where there are no partings." If Catholic women in the latter part of the nineteenth century gained a "new freedom of religious expression," this "emotional devotionalism" may well have spilled over into the way some women understood their secular life.[90] The "wicked life" may refer specifically to her own violation of moral codes, but if she was following the teachings of her church, the statement would be inclusive, as true for those who appeared respectable as it was for herself. A woman who sinned in a "wicked" world, Alice seems nevertheless to have believed that love, fidelity, and devotion—the essence of her bond with Channing—would redeem the pair.

One lonely night in Channing's apartment, Alice read a book, "our 'Science of Life.' "[91] There are several works with this title. In 1870 Orson Squire Fowler wrote *Creative and Sexual Science*, also called *Science of Life*, a phrenological guide to sex and marriage; Robert Charles Hannon's *Science of Life and Power of Our Mind*, on mental healing, appeared in 1894. It is conceivable that Alice was reading one of these volumes: her letters offer no specific evidence of an orientation to phrenology or Christian Science, but Alice did complain frequently of physical ailments and mental uneasiness, went often to physicians, and may have turned to one of these books for guidance.

It seems more likely, however, that she was reading a book by that name written in 1904 by Pearl Mary Craigie, an Anglo-

American novelist and dramatist. Addressing the problems of modernity, Craigie considered how individuals should live in a world of boundless energy, never-ending work, and new amusements and temptations. She wrote:

> [J]ust as people never worked as they work now, they were never before so eager as they are at the present day to have luxuries and pleasures and enjoyments of every kind—and they are desperate, often without knowing it, because . . . they have this feeling . . . that if they do not get some prize here, and immediately to show for their pains, they may never get anything at all.

Craigie discussed young people whose romantic dreams clashed with the reality of life. Criticizing "sham refinement," she observed that true joy did not come from material possessions or the desire to advance beyond one's station. What then was happiness? "A good inherent in the soul, but the object that makes one happy is something outside the soul." Offering a gloss on Saint Thomas Aquinas, she reiterated, "we all have the capacity for happiness, but . . . we cannot, by ourselves, or unaided, be happy." Such happiness would come about, Craigie observed, not through large-scale social reforms, but rather through "attention to the individual."[92]

Whoever suggested she read the volume—a sibling, friend, perhaps a priest—knew the dilemmas of Alice Hanley's life. Dissatisfied with her station, absorbed with appearances, and often desperately lonely, Alice must have seen herself in Craigie's prose. Without directly attributing her thoughts to her reading *The Science of Life*, Alice goes on in the same letter to reflect upon its theme: "You know Chan that a great deal of my happiness depends on you as I know you were always ready to advise me & I think I would never be the same if I had lost your affection." Alice here restated Craigie's other-directed psychology that "you cannot have too much attention, too much care," but also imagined Channing's retort, grounded in a more Victorian view of human character: "I suppose you will say I am selfish, well perhaps I am." Alice must have considered this subject important: she composed a draft before writing this passage into her letter.[93]

❖

Alice imagined her future with Channing when she wrote about an omen, "[s]omething seems to be foreshown to me." Noting how "very lonesome" Channing was at the Mundale construction site, she reassured him, "I think we will be soon together forever." The actual portent, freedom from financial worry, dependency, and separation, was prosaic enough. "Perhaps after a while you could get a job some place where I could help you out even for my board & a little to help get things." Acknowledging the difficulties Channing faced in the workplace, she hoped that "[p]erhaps some day you wont have to work like you are now." She dreamed of becoming "the proprietors of something ourself some day," a vision of small-scale ownership that permitted independence, family, and dignity to flourish. But the dream remained beyond their grasp.[94]

In the last letters, Alice's illnesses (and possibly the pregnancy), her poverty, and Channing's anger and suspicion lent a disillusioned and resentful note to her writing. Calling herself "cranky" and "nervous," Alice began to see her love almost as a mental disorder. "Oh Chan dont mind me for I know I have got to think so much of you I really think it has worked on my mind," she wrote. On several occasions she wrote about death, including a doggerel poem asking Channing to "remember me . . . when I am far above." In the summer of 1908, having returned to Northampton, she described a variety of painful symptoms, contemplated suicide (although it is difficult to say how seriously), and started to make a pillow for Channing as a token of remembrance. It may be that she was pregnant and nearing term. She now worked laundering clothes for people Channing knew. "I am so lame I can hardly stir my arms," she wrote, but "I must try & do something." Bitterly dwelling on Channing's accusations, she had set out to repay him: "Hope you are well & enjoying life while the *tramp* is gone[,] but never mind I wont always be one I hope."[95]

Although the letters cover barely thirteen months, Alice Hanley and Channing Lewis remained together for seven more years. She continued to live at home—or at least maintained that illusion—through 1912, but she spent much of her time in Springfield. In 1910 federal census takers recorded Alice Hanley both at her parents' house in Northampton and at Channing's apartment in Springfield. Stating her unhappiness when apart from Channing, Alice had conceded only one exception: "I do love to see mamma & know she is all right." In 1912 or 1913, Alice permanently "removed to Springfield." For a brief period she resided apart from Channing, who boarded with a relative, but from 1913 to 1915, they lived together in an apartment on Worthington Street.

These years were troubled ones for the Hanley family. James continued to work in Newton at least until 1913. John and his wife, Mary Scully Hanley, living at the Bright Avenue house, had problems early in their marriage: Mary petitioned the court in 1913 for custody of their son "as they are living apart" but the two reconciled not long after. Then Alice's mother, who had stayed at Bright Avenue as head of household, died on New Year's Day in 1914 "after a long illness." In 1916, James returned to the area, boarding with Katharine and David Hoar in Springfield. [96]

Whatever the depth of Alice's feelings for Channing—"once I love it is forever"—the two separated in 1916. Alice moved to a rooming house nearby where Thomas Brennan, a twenty-nine-year-old Irish American metal lather, also boarded. Soon thereafter the two married. Alice was now forty but, perhaps sensing an unseemliness in the marriage, they reported only a five-year age difference on the marriage license. No record reveals the nature of their union: whether, as the circumstances seem to suggest, she married on the rebound and he for convenience. Although they rented, Alice called herself a "rooming house proprietor" who presumably cooked, cleaned, and washed for boarders. In 1917, the Brennans adopted a son. Now a wife and mother, Alice achieved the form of what she had craved in her letters to Channing, but its substance eluded her. As the property and probate records indicate, Alice's father continued to shun her even after her marriage. Moreover, the pain, sickness, and gynecological problems Alice referred to in the letters probably continued through this time. In 1920 she was diagnosed with uterine cancer: a doctor began to attend her in the summer of that year, but she died in December. The contributory cause of death, the doctor noted, was exhaustion.[97]

Alice's obituary in the Springfield newspaper named her the "wife of Thomas F. Brennan." The Northampton paper, in contrast, identified Mrs. Thomas Brennan as "formerly Miss Alice Hanley of this city," survived by her father, brother, and sister, with no mention of Alice's husband or child. The funeral and Mass were held in Springfield, but she was buried in Northampton, in the family plot. Thomas Brennan waited the customary year of mourning before remarrying.[98] Alice Hanley slipped into the obscurity of history until the serendipitous discovery of her black lace stocking.

❧

This may be a story of forbidden love, but it is a story framed in oddly conventional terms. As the color line was drawn more sharply, public discourses of the time cast intimacy between black men and white women as a perversion of the moral and social order. In terms of those discourses, Alice Hanley's transgressions were many, as she crossed racial boundaries, engaged in nonmarital sex, and defied the authority of her father. Seen by others, perhaps, as a "disorderly woman," Alice understood herself differently, her sins forgivable because her actions were dictated by love. We can see that for Alice, whatever questions interracial sexuality raised were deeply embedded, if not buried, in the particularities of working-class life for women. She was caught in webs of economic, familial, and psychological dependency and she had few resources with which to extract herself from them. She felt acutely the cultural imperatives of female respectability and virtue. These considerations, and her transcendent love for Channing, were most palpable to her. Alice Hanley's letters, as difficult and ambiguous as they are, reveal some of the complex and unexpected ways people grasp and negotiate the ethical choices in sexual relationships culturally proscribed as taboo.

## NOTES

I am indebted to Paul Gaffney, whose meticulous and thoughtful research enabled me to interpret these letters. I also thank Miriam Rosen, Elise Feeley, Lynne Bassett, Meg Hannigan, Maggie Lowe, Elaine Parmet, Alan Derickson, Frank Faulkner, and Judith Leavitt for their help with specific research questions; the University of Massachusetts Library, Connecticut Valley Historical Museum, Northampton Historical Society, and Forbes Library; and Peter Agree, Carroll Smith-Rosenberg, and my 1994 U.S. women's history graduate seminar for comments on earlier versions of this essay.

1   Twenty-seven letters from Alice Hanley to Channing Lewis [hereafter AH to CL], dated 2 August 1907 to 17 August 1908, and three letters from Mike Manning to Alice Hanley, 25 November to 16 December 1902, were found at 15 Bright Avenue, Northampton, Massachusetts, and are in the possession of Pamela See.

2   Martha Elizabeth Hodes, "Sex across the Color Line: White Women and Black Men in the Nineteenth Century American South" (Ph.D. diss., Princeton University, 1991); Peggy Pascoe, "Race, Gender, and Intercultural Relations: The Case of Interracial Marriage," *Frontiers* 12, no. 1 (1991): 5–18. See also Paul R. Spickard, *Mixed Blood: Intermarriage and Ethnic Identity in Twentieth Century America* (Madison: University of Wisconsin Press, 1989); John D'Emilio and Estelle Freedman, *Intimate Matters: A History of Sexuality in America* (New York: Harper and Row, 1988).

3   Ida B. Wells-Barnett, *On Lynching* (1892; reprint, New York: Arno, 1969). For an example in a national women's magazine of the racist ideology Wells

combatted, see Ellen Barret Ligon, "The White Woman and the Negro," *Good Housekeeping*, November 1903, 426–29.

4  Al-Tony Gilmore, "Jack Johnson and White Women: The National Impact," *Journal of Negro History* 58 (January 1973): 18–38 (quote on 32).

5  David H. Fowler, *Northern Attitudes Towards Interracial Marriages: Legislation and Public Opinion in the Middle Atlantic and the States of the Old Northwest, 1780–1930* (1963; New York: Garland, 1987), see especially 215, 273–75, 285; Spickard, *Mixed Blood*, 272; Julius Drachsler, *Intermarriage in New York City*, Studies in History, Economics, and Public Law, No. 213 (New York: Columbia University Press, 1921), 43, 49–50; Olivier Zunz, *The Changing Face of Inequality: Urbanization, Industrial Development and Immigrants in Detroit, 1880–1920* (Chicago: University of Chicago Press, 1983), 245. On gay interracial interactions, see George Chauncey, *Gay New York: Gender, Urban Culture, and the Making of the Gay Male World, 1890–1940* (New York: Basic Books, 1994).

6  See, e.g., David Roediger, *The Wages of Whiteness* (New York: Verso, 1991); Graham Hodges, " 'Desirable Companions and Lovers': Irish and African Americans in the Sixth Ward, 1830–1870," in *The New York Irish*, ed. Ron Bayor and Timothy Meagher (Baltimore: Johns Hopkins University Press, 1996).

7  Evelyn Brooks Higginbotham, "African-American Women's History and the Metalanguage of Race," *Signs* 17 (Winter 1992): 251–74.

8  This account is pieced together from public documents and Hanley family stories about their ancestors; these records are fragmentary and conflicting. See U.S. Bureau of the Census, *Ninth Census of the United States, 1870, Population Schedules*, Pittsfield, Massachusetts, 86; U.S. Bureau of the Census, *Twelfth Census of the United States, 1900, Population Schedules*, Northampton, Massachusetts, Enumeration District 630, sheet 3; Death certificate of James Hanley, 23 May 1931, Springfield City Clerk's Office. Interview with Teressia Hanley by Paul Gaffney, August 1993. No definitive information on James Hanley's emigration from Ireland has been found. The name Hanley, alternatively Handley or in Gaellic *Ohainle*, originated in Connacht, the western part of County Cork, one of the poorest regions in Ireland. See Edward Maclysaght, *Surnames of Ireland* (Dublin: Irish Academic Press, 1988), 145.

Alice Ryan and her family are particularly obscure: Thomas Ryan, age twenty-five, is listed as boarding with John W. Hanley in the 1870 U.S. Census; Alice Ryan's father is also named Thomas. On the Hoosac Tunnel, see William Bond Wheelwright, *Life and Times of Alvah Crocker* (Boston: Douglas Crocker, 1923).

9  Marriage Register, James Hanley and Alice Ryan, 25 July 1871, *Pittsfield Vital Statistics*, 3: 2. *Pittsfield Directory for the Year 1869* (Pittsfield: John B. Haskins,

1869), 55; *Pittsfield Directory*, 1873, 1875, and 1876; Death certificate of Alice M. Ryan Hanley, 1 January 1914, Northampton, Hampshire County; Frederick W. Beers, *County Atlas of Berkshire, Massachusetts* (New York: R. T. White, 1876); interview with James and Betty Hanley, 27 June 1994.

Records disagree on the age difference between Alice Ryan and James Hanley: their gravestone indicates a difference of two years; their marriage record five years. However, James Hanley's date of birth both in the 1900 U.S. Census and on his death certificate is 1854. If Alice Ryan was born in 1846, as the 1900 U.S. Census and marriage register indicate, their age difference would have been eight years. On marriage patterns among Irish immigrants, see Hasia Diner, *Erin's Daughters in America: Irish Immigrant Women in the Nineteenth Century* (Baltimore: Johns Hopkins University Press, 1983), 4–7, 46–51.

10  U.S. Bureau of the Census, *Tenth Census of the United States, 1880, Population Schedules*, Weston, Massachusetts, Enumeration District No. 383, 39; *Twelfth Census, 1900, Population Schedules*, Northampton; U.S. Bureau of the Census, *Thirteenth Census of the United States, 1910, Population Schedules*, Northampton, Massachusetts, Enumeration District 695, sheet 3. Record of birth of Alice Hanley, 25 August 1875, Pittsfield, Berkshire County; Record of birth of Catherine [sic] Hanley, 31 July 1877, Weston, Middlesex County; F. W. Beers, *County Atlas of Middlesex County* (New York: J. B. Beers, 1875), 86. This essay spells Katharine Hanley's name as she did, although official records offer variant spellings.

11  Tercentenary History Committee, ed., *The Northampton Book* (Northampton: Tercentenary Committee, 1954); see especially Harold U. Faulkner, "How Our People Lived," 273–76, and Archibald V. Galbraith, "Industrial History: 1860–1900," 233–39; Phyllis Maud Freeman, "Industrial and Labor Developments in the City of Northampton, Massachusetts, 1898 to 1930" (M.A. thesis, Smith College, 1931); Massachusetts Bureau of Statistics of Labor, *Labor Bulletin* no. 16 (November 1900): 141; Charles J. Dean, "The Mills of Mill River" (1935), typescript in Forbes Library, Northampton; Albert H. Carpenter, "Northampton, Past and Present," *Western New England* 1, no. 11 (October 1911); *Daily Hampshire Gazette*, Tenth Anniversary Number, 20 December 1900. On the reform tradition, see Christopher Clark, *The Communitarian Moment: The Radical Challenge of the Northampton Association* (Ithaca: Cornell University Press, 1995).

12  Frederick D. Meehan, "The Growth and Development of the Parochial School System in Northampton, Massachusetts, 1891–1949" (M.A. thesis, Smith College, 1949), 3–4; Frederick Cusick, "The Irish: Their Settling Here Largely Without Strife," *Daily Hampshire Gazette*, 16 March 1977.

13  John Francis Manfredi, "Immigration to Northampton," in Tercentenary History Committee, *Northampton Book*, 331–36; Massachusetts *Labor Bulletin*, no. 21 (February 1902): 14–15. On tenements, see *Daily Hampshire Gazette*, Tenth Anniversary Number, 20 December 1900; Massachusetts Bureau of Labor Statistics, *Census of Massachusetts 1895*, 7 vols. (Boston: Wright and Potter, 1896), 4: 601. On social conditions of the immigrant poor, see Chief of Police, *Twenty-fifth Annual Report*, in Northampton, *City Reports* (1908), 314; Northampton School Committee, *Twenty-fifth Annual Report* (Northampton, 1908); Overseers of the Poor of the City of Northampton, *Twenty-sixth Annual Report* (Northampton: Herald Job Printers, 1910); Lynn Slaughter, "The Impact of Immigration on the History of Northampton, Massachusetts" (1969), typescript in Forbes Library, 70, 75–78, 88–92. Reform efforts in Northampton are documented in the People's Institute Papers, Forbes Library, Northampton; Hampshire Regional Young Men's Christian Association Papers, Special Collections, University of Massachusetts at Amherst.

14  William W. Millett, "The Irish and Mobility Patterns in Northampton, Massachusetts, 1846–1888" (Ph.D. diss., University of Iowa, 1980), especially 162–71, 180–83, 207–13, 220–25, 274–79; Cusick, "The Irish"; Meehan, "Growth and Development," 15; Candice Conrad, "A Study of the Comparative Occupational Mobility of Five Ethnic Groups in Northampton, 1920–1962" (1969), typescript in Forbes Library. See also Katherine Ellen McCarthy, "Psychiatry in the Nineteenth Century: The Early Years of Northampton State Hospital" (Ph.D. diss., University of Pennsylvania, 1974), on the disproportionate confinement of the Irish as mental patients. For a call for religious tolerance, see *Daily Hampshire Gazette*, 19 September 1900.

15  Richard C. Garvey, "The Roman Catholic Church in Northampton" (n.d.), typescript in Forbes Library; Margaret Clifford Dwyer, *Centennial History of St. Mary of the Assumption Church, Northampton, Mass. 1866–1966* (South Hackensack, N.J.: Custombook, 1966); Virginia Corwin, "Religious Life in Northampton, 1800–1954," in Tercentenary History Committee, *Northampton Book*, 383–93; Meehan, "Growth and Development"; Millett, "Irish and Mobility Patterns," 259 n.11; Slaughter, "Impact of Immigration," 116.

16  Dwyer, *Centennial History of St. Mary's*; *Daily Hampshire Gazette*, 23 May 1931; *Northampton and Easthampton Directory, 1893–1894* (Northampton: Price and Lee Co., 1892), 82.

17  Christopher Adams's listings in *Northampton Directory* for the years 1894 to 1898; *Daily Hampshire Gazette*, 25 May 1931. Michael J. Shea, ed., *A Century of Catholicism in Western Massachusetts* (Springfield: Mirror Press, 1931), 270–71.

18  St. Michael's School, Northampton, Massachusetts, Register 1891–1904,

Forbes Library. Millett, "Irish and Mobility Patterns," 216–17; Northampton School Committee, *Annual Report*, 1885–86, quoted in Slaughter, "Impact of Immigration," 75.

19 Meehan, "Growth and Development," 20–22, 40.

20 On Blodgett, see *Dictionary of American Biography* (New York: Charles Scribner's Sons, 1929), 2: 381–82; L. Clark Seelye, *The Early History of Smith College, 1871–1910* (Boston: Houghton Mifflin Co., 1923), 55–56. *Daily Hampshire Gazette*, 3 May 1881; 26 July 1893; Fifth Anniversary Supplement, 30 November 1895; 30 April 1904. *Atlas of the City of Northampton and Town of Easthampton* (Philadelphia: D. L. Miller & Co., 1895); *Northampton and Easthampton Directory*, 1893–1894, 35.

21 *Pittsfield Directory*, 1873, 23, 50, 126; F. W. Beers, *County Atlas of Berkshire*; *St. Joseph's Parish Golden Jubilee*, 1849–1899, Pittsfield, Mass. Souvenir (c.1899); *Daily Hampshire Gazette*, 26 July 1893; *Newton Directory*, 1905, 278.

22 George Washington Cable, "The Home-Culture Clubs," *World's Work* 12 (October 1906): 8112.

23 Hampshire County Registry of Deeds, Book 498, 5 May 1897, 97–98; Book 498, 6 May 1897, 421–22. Mark T. Mason in *Northampton and Easthampton Directory*, 1893–94, 109; *Atlas of the City of Northampton*; Sanborn Map Company, Fire Insurance Maps, Northampton, Massachusetts, 1884, 1889, 1895, Geography and Map Division, Library of Congress (microfilm ed., 1981).

24 *Twelfth Census, 1900, Population Schedules*, Northampton; *Thirteenth Census, 1910, Population Schedules*, Northampton; Katharine Hanley's listings in *Northampton Directory* for the years 1899 to 1910; St. Michael's School Register. On the mobility of second-generation Irish women, see Diner, *Erin's Daughters*, 77–98. For Boston wages, see *Massachusetts Labor Bulletin*, no. 46 (February 1907): 77; no. 47 (March 1907): 164–65.

25 American International College, which holds the records of the Northampton Commercial College going back at least to 1902–1903, has no record for John or Katharine Hanley; before 1898, however, the commercial college only offered individual instruction and may not have kept transcripts. A Hanley descendant remembers John's diploma from the college. James and Betty Hanley interview; Roland F. Aubin to author, 7 July 1994; *250th Anniversary Guide and Business Directory* (Northampton: Warner & Eisold, 1904), 15; *Northampton Directory*, 1896–97, inside front cover; Meehan, "Growth and Development," 23.

26 Charles Forbes Warner, *Representative Families of Northampton: A Demonstration of What High Character, Good Ancestry and Heredity Have Accomplished in a New England Town*, vol. 1 (Northampton: Picturesque Publishing Co., 1917), 84–92;

Home Culture Clubs, Board of Directors, Minutes 1896–1909, 1 vol., People's Institute Papers, see 2 November 1896. On women, office work, and secretarial training, see Sharon Hartman Strom, *Beyond the Typewriter: Gender, Class and the Origins of Modern American Office Work* (Urbana: University of Illinois Press, 1992); Walter Licht, *Getting Work: Philadelphia, 1840–1950* (Cambridge: Harvard University Press, 1992); Ileen DeVault, *Sons and Daughters of Labor: Class and Clerical Work in Turn-of-the-Century Pittsburgh* (Ithaca: Cornell University Press, 1990).

27 Alice Hanley does not appear in the *Northampton Directory* for the years from 1893 to 1905; she is listed as "boarding" but without an occupation from 1906 to 1913. The 1900 and 1910 U.S. Census list her in Northampton without an occupation. In her letter of 29 April 1908, she mentions that she "will go in & work to morrrow & Sat.," apparently a casual or temporary job. By summer of 1908, she was earning some money washing clothes.

28 Figures calculated from *Census of Massachusetts*, 1895, 4: 68–71, 578–83. See also Massachusetts Bureau of Labor Statistics, *Census of Massachusetts, 1885*, 3 vols. (Boston: Wright and Potter, 1885), vol. 1, part 2, 204–7; Massachusetts Bureau of Labor Statistics, *Census of Massachusetts*, 1905, 4 vols. (Boston: Wright and Potter, 1910), 2: 207–9. Marjorie Ruzich Abel, "Profiles of Nineteenth Century Working Women," *Historical Journal of Massachusetts* 14 (January 1986): 43–52. For a general discussion of Irish women's work, see Diner, *Erin's Daughters*.

29 AH to CL, 17 May 1908; 6 May 1908. James and Betty Hanley interview.

30 U.S. Bureau of the Census, *Tenth Census of the United States, 1880, Population Schedules*, Springfield, Massachusetts; U.S. Bureau of the Census, *Twelfth Census of the United States, 1900, Population Schedules*, Springfield, Massachusetts, Enumeration District 589, sheet 7. Records of birth of Grace C. Lewis, 6 November 1882, and Channing M. Lewis (son), 4 March 1884; Record of death of Amelia Peters Lewis, 11 August 1884, Book 1884, 71; Marriage record of Channing M. Lewis and Josephine Murphy, 27 May 1890, all in Springfield City Clerk's Office. Lewis appears in both Springfield and Northampton in 1896–1897. *Springfield Directory* for the years 1896 to 1899 (Springfield: Price and Lee, 1896–99); *Northampton Directory* for the years 1896 to 1898.

31 *Springfield Directory* for the years 1902 and 1903.

32 Mike Manning to Alice Hanley, 25 November, 16 December 1902; *Holyoke City Directory*, 1903 (Holyoke: Price and Lee, 1903), 260.

33 An idea of Northampton's commercial culture can be gleaned from *Daily Hampshire Gazette* advertising and *Northampton Directory* business directories in these years. See also Tercentenary History Committee, *Northampton Book*.

34  Daily Hampshire Gazette, 20 December 1900; 5 September 1900. Springfield Direc-
    tory, 1908, 777–78; Carpenter, "Northampton: Past and Present," 357. Persis
    Putnam, "The Trolley-Car Era: 1901–1918," in Tercentenary History Com-
    mittee, Northampton Book, 305; Robert A. Young, "The Mount Tom Electric
    Railway," Historical Journal of Massachusetts 13 (January 1985): 43–44.

35  Chauncey, Gay New York, 257–67; Kathy Peiss, "Gender, Class, Race and the
    Geography of Urban Leisure," paper presented at the Joint Hungarian-
    American Conference on New York and Budapest History, Hungarian Acad-
    emy of Sciences, August 1988.

36  AH to CL, 6 May 1908; "City Items," Daily Hampshire Gazette, 4 April 1908;
    Hennessey Three Star Cigars advertisement, Daily Hampshire Gazette, 27 January
    1906.

37  See David Hoar's and Channing Lewis's listings in Northampton Directory, 1907;
    Springfield Directory for the years 1896 to 1900, 1903, 1905. On Bartenders'
    Local #113 in Northampton, see Freeman, "Industrial and Labor Develop-
    ments," 76, 81, 260. On the Nelson Hotel, see AH to CL, 22 November
    1907; advertisement in Springfield Directory, 1902, 1053. Lewis's "connections"
    are suggested by the fact that he secured a job as cook to engineers and
    contractors overseeing a massive public works project, described in Springfield
    Republican, 3 May 1908; Pasquale A. Breglio, the contractor who supplied the
    unskilled labor for the project, was, not coincidentally, proprietor of a
    saloon and restaurant (Springfield Directory, 1905, 79).

38  AH to CL, 2 August 1907.

39  AH to CL, 22 November 1907; on Mary A. Ryan, see Twelfth Census, 1900,
    Population Schedules, Northampton; Northampton Directory, 1907, 158.

40  On the black population of Northampton, see Massachusetts Labor Bulletin,
    no. 21 (February 1902): 14–15. Daily Hampshire Gazette, 8 May 1908; 25
    September 1909; see also 5 June 1900; 8 April 1908; 15 May 1908.

41  AH to CL, 1 June 1908. "Lewis" listing in Westfield Directory, 1905 (Springfield:
    Price and Lee Co., 1905).

42  AH to CL, 17 August 1908. Hampshire County Registry of Deeds, Book
    595, 25 April 1905, 235–36; Northampton Directory for the years 1893 to
    1923; Newton Directory (biannual), for the years 1905 to 1913, except 1907.
    Thirteenth Census, 1910, Population Schedules, Northampton, lists Alice Ryan Han-
    ley as the head of household; James Hanley does not appear. On Blodgett's
    departure, see Northampton Directory, 1904; "Benjamin Colman Blodgett," Dic-
    tionary of American Biography.

43  AH to CL, 19 December 1907; 6 May 1908; 25 May 1908.

44  Hampshire County Registry of Deeds, Book 595, 25 April 1905, 235–36;

Book 686, 31 December 1912, 424; Book 712, 20 May 1915, 449, 455, 461–2; Book 750, 22 September 1919, 189; Book 750, 6 October 1919, 443, 527.

45  On Alice's marriage, adoption of a son, and James's response, see Marriage record of Alice M. Hanley and Thomas F. Brennan, 10 May 1916, Springfield City Clerk's Office; Certificate of baptism and registrum of James Francis Brennan, 16 September 1923, Sacred Heart Church, Springfield; U.S. Bureau of the Census, *Fourteenth Census of the United States*, 1920, *Population Schedules*, Springfield, Massachusetts, Enumeration District 98, sheet 2; Will of James Hanley, 26 December 1925, and Probate Inventory, 16 June 1931, in Hampshire County Registry of Probate.

46  AH to CL, 17 May 1908; 2 June 1908; 24 December 1907.

47  AH to CL, 1 June 1908; 19 May 1908; 17 May 1908; 2 August 1907; 27 April 1908.

48  AH to CL, 19 December 1907. Although her language indicates that this was a pregnancy, it is possible that she had contracted venereal disease.

49  Ibid. On working-class women and pregnancy, Judith Walzer Leavitt, personal communication, 14 June 1994. On hospital policy, see Cooley Dickinson Hospital, *Report of the Trustees* (Northampton: Gazette Printing Co., 1908). Also serving maternity cases in Northampton was "Mrs. Sparks' private hospital," but I have found no detailed information on it (*Daily Hampshire Gazette*, 12 October 1907).

50  James and Betty Hanley interview. Although the adoption records are closed, it does not appear that Alice adopted her own baby (which Channing fathered) in 1917. Recounting the family story, the Hanleys distinguished between the "dark" baby and the Brennan son, who is also listed as "white" in the 1920 Census Population Schedules.

51  AH to CL, 20 July 1908. On the meanings of the term "sick" in this period, Leavitt, personal communication.

52  AH to CL, 10 April 1908; 17 August 1908; 28 June 1908.

53  AH to CL, 19 December 1907.

54  Ibid.

55  Katharine Hanley listings in *Northampton Directory* for the years 1901 to 1911; *Twelfth Census*, 1900, *Population Schedules*, Northampton; *Thirteenth Census*, 1910, *Population Schedules*, Northampton; marriage certificate of David John Hoar and Katharine Teresa Hanley, 23 November 1909, New York City. See also Diner, *Erin's Daughters*, 77–98.

56  Last Will and Testament of Oliver Smith, 22 December 1845; *Daily Hampshire Gazette*, 30 April 1907; Smith Charities, *Sixty-first Annual Report* (Northampton, 1909).

57  *Hampshire Gazette* [weekly], 15 November 1887; *Northampton Daily Herald*, 4 February 1894 clipping, in Annual Meeting Minutes, 1891–1917, YMCA Papers; *Daily Hampshire Gazette*, Fifth Anniversary Supplement, 30 November 1895.

58  See Philip Butcher, *George Washington Cable: The Northampton Years* (New York: Columbia University Press, 1959), 72–91; Cable, "The Home-Culture Clubs," 8110–114. *Home Culture Club Letter*, 1893–95; Home Culture Clubs [People's Institute], *Yearbook*, 1898–1910, in People's Institute Papers. *Hampshire Gazette* [weekly], 15 February 1887. In addition to Blodgett and Williston, who were founders, Edwin B. Emerson, John Hanley's first employer, was a donor and fund-raiser for the Home Culture Clubs.

59  Home Culture Clubs, *Yearbook*, 1900, 13; *Yearbook*, 1908–1909, 7–8; Cable, "Home-Culture Clubs," 8114; *Daily Hampshire Gazette*, 27 November 1899, clipping, in Home Culture Clubs, *Scrapbook*, 1889–1902, People's Institute Papers. On Smith College students' involvement, see *Smith College Monthly*, June 1895, 24–26; Edith Brill, volume of letters, 29 November 1896, 9 December 1896, 5 February 1897, 1 April 1897, in Smith College Archives, Northampton.

60  Galbraith, "Industrial History," 238; *Daily Hampshire Gazette*, 20 September 1900, 12 May 1908; Diner, *Erin's Daughters*, 114.

61  *Home Culture Club Letter* 1 (January 1893): 1–3; ibid. 3 (October 1894): 1–3; ibid. 3 (November 1894): 2. Freeman, "Industrial and Labor Developments," 15, 28–37. For a view of "Florence girls" at a city celebration, see *The Meadow City's Quarter-Millennial Book 5–7 June 1904* (Northampton, [ca. 1904]), 287, 261.

62  *Home Culture Club Letter* 1 (January 1893): 1. One People's Institute history suggests that working women had already been meeting in clubs when George Washington Cable decided to establish the organization. See "The People's Institute," 1942 typescript, box 7, folder 67, People's Institute Papers.

63  *Daily Hampshire Gazette*, 19 September 1900.

64  *Daily Hampshire Gazette*, 2 June and 6 June 1899, clippings in Home Culture Clubs, *Scrapbook*.

65  *Daily Hampshire Gazette*, 21 and 22 November 1906.

66  See, e.g., Kiely-Ahearn wedding notice, *Daily Hampshire Gazette*, 6 January 1909.

67  Marriage certificate of David Hoar and Katharine Hanley. On Catholic church marriage requirements at this time, see Charles Herberman et al., eds., *The Catholic Encyclopedia*, 15 vols. (New York: Robert Appleton, 1908), 4: 3.

68  My thanks to Maggie Lowe for this observation.

69  AH to CL, 17 August 1908; 19 December 1907; 22 November 1907. On working women and sexual morality, see Kathy Peiss, " 'Charity Girls' and City Pleasures: Historical Notes on Working Class Sexuality, 1880–1920," in *Powers of Desire: The Politics of Sexuality*, ed. Ann Snitow et al. (New York: Monthly Review Press, 1983), 74–87.

70  AH to CL, 19 December 1907.

71  AH to CL, 22 April 1908.

72  Clothing advertisements, *Daily Hampshire Gazette*, April 1908; see especially 3 April 1908, 2. In 1907, weekly wages for cooks in Boston, likely higher than those in Springfield, ranged from five to seventeen dollars, with the average about eleven dollars: Massachusetts *Labor Bulletin*, no. 46 (February 1907): 77.

73  There were also 310 dressmakers in Springfield. *Springfield Directory*, 1908, 633, 641–44.

74  "Among the Dressmakers," *Daily Hampshire Gazette*, 12 June 1891; "To Sew a Fine Seam: Northampton Dressmakers, 1880–1905," Historic Northampton exhibit, May 1993. Lynne Bassett provided useful information on local dressmakers, fashions, and prices in the period.

75  *Daily Hampshire Gazette*, 31 December 1908; 8 January 1909; 9 January 1909. AH to CL, 25 May 1908.

76  AH to CL, 25 May 1908; 27 April 1908, 17 May 1908. On the importance of dress to working-class women, see Diner, *Erin's Daughters*, 141; Christine Stansell, *City of Women* (New York: Knopf, 1986); Kathy Peiss, *Cheap Amusements: Working Women and Leisure in Turn-of-the-Century New York* (Philadelphia: Temple University Press, 1986), 56–87.

77  AH to CL, 1 June 1908.

78  AH to CL, 17 May 1908; 15 May 1908.

79  AH to CL, 21 May 1908.

80  AH to CL, 24 December 1907; 10 April 1908. "Retail Prices in Massachusetts for Articles of Household Consumption—October 1907," Massachusetts *Labor Bulletin*, no. 55 (December 1907): 225–39, provides prices in various cities in the state, including Springfield.

81  AH to CL, 29 April 1908; 21 May 1908.

82  U.S. Bureau of the Census, *Thirteenth Census of the United States, 1910, Population Schedules*, Springfield, Massachusetts, Enumeration District 620, sheet 3; AH to CL, 2 June 1908; 3 June 1908.

83  AH to CL, 10 April 1908; 2 June 1908.

84  *Springfield Republican*, 3 May 1908; AH to CL, 22 April 1908. Although there may have been no "camp followers" at the Little River site, there was pros-

titution in the Springfield-Holyoke area. See Karen A. Terrell, "Exposure of Prostitution in Western Massachusetts: 1911," *Historical Journal of Massachusetts* 8 (June 1980): 3–11.

85  AH to CL, 17 May 1908; 21 May 1908; 28 June 1908.

86  AH to CL, 15 May 1908; *Daily Hampshire Gazette*, 9 May 1909. Interview with Margaret Clifford Dwyer by Paul Gaffney, 4 March 1994. On women in Catholic organizations, see Diner, *Erin's Daughters*, 120–37.

87  AH to CL, 1 June 1908. *Hampshire Gazette* [weekly], 6 December 1887; 29 November 1887; 21 February 1888. *Daily Hampshire Gazette*, 19 March 1907; 31 May 1907. Patrick F. McSweeney, "Old-Time Temperance Societies," *Catholic World* 62 (January 1896): 482–86. On saloon culture, see Roy Rosenzweig, *Eight Hours for What We Will* (Cambridge: Cambridge University Press, 1983).

88  Joseph F. Doherty, *Moral Problems of Interracial Marriage* (Washington: Catholic University of America, 1949), 24–31. Herberman, *The Catholic Encyclopedia*, 9: 698–99. See also Leslie Woodcock Tentler, "On the Margins: The State of American Catholic History," *American Quarterly* 45 (March 1993): 104–27.

89  AH to CL, 1 June 1908; 21 May 1908. On the de-emphasis of romance in Irish culture, see Diner, *Erin's Daughters*, 23, 58. On romantic love in workingwomen's culture, see Dorothy Richardson, *The Long Day* (1905) in *Women at Work*, ed. William L. O'Neill (New York: Times Books, 1972); Peiss, *Cheap Amusements*.

90  AH to CL, 1 June 1908. Tentler, "On the Margins," 116.

91  AH to CL, 27 April 1908.

92  Mrs. P[earl Mary] Craigie, *The Science of Life* (New York: Scott-Thaw Co., 1904), 8–9, 66–67, 48–57.

93  AH to CL, 27 April 1908.

94  AH to CL, 2 June 1908, 1 June 1908.

95  AH to CL, 20 July 1908; 17 August 1908.

96  *Newton Directory*, 1913, and 1915; *Springfield Directory*, 1916. Hampshire County Registry of Probate, Box 374, 23 September 1913; Box 379, 2 December 1913. *Daily Hampshire Gazette*, 1 January 1914, 3.

97  *Fourteenth Census, 1920, Population Schedules*, Springfield; Marriage record of Alice Hanley and Thomas Brennan; Certificate of baptism of James Francis Brennan; Record of death of Alice Hanley, 15 December 1920, Springfield City Clerk's Office.

98  *Springfield Daily Republican*, 15 December 1920; *Daily Hampshire Gazette*, 14 December 1920; 17 December 1920. Certificate of marriage of Thomas Francis B[re]nnan and Alice Edith (Hosley) Way, 21 December 1921, Springfield.

# THE SPRINGFIELD OF
# CHANNING LEWIS,
# A COLORED MAN

Louis Wilson

Who was Channing Lewis? Unlike his lover, Alice Hanley, he left no letters—or at least none that have yet been discovered—recording his thoughts and feelings. What we know about him we know only indirectly and incompletely, by extrapolating from Alice's words and from a variety of official documents—city directories, church and association records, census data, and deeds—that mention Lewis and other members of his family.

From these sources we learn, for example, that Channing Lewis was born in Lawrenceville, Virginia, probably in 1862 or 1863—perhaps born into slavery under Confederate law despite President Abraham Lincoln's signing of the Emancipation Proclamation. Records further indicate that Lewis first came to Springfield in 1879 or 1880, joining in the significant migration of southern blacks that began with the collapse of Reconstruction in 1877. As the federal government abandoned its efforts to guarantee equal rights for southern "Negroes," and as violence by whites against former slaves intensified, ever-growing numbers of freed blacks left the South in search of a better way of life. Some went to the Midwest—to Chicago, Detroit, St. Louis, and Kansas City—where they established their own separate communities. Others moved to the thriving industrial centers of mid-Atlantic and northeastern states— Philadelphia, Newark, New York.[1]

In escaping the South these newly freed men and women hoped to find not only a measure of legal and political equality, but also greater personal security and economic opportunity. A legacy of abolitionism, including the efforts of those who brought fugitive slaves North via the Underground Railroad, may have made some towns, like Springfield, seem especially inviting. There were other inducements as well (such as free public education), which were unavailable to blacks in the South.

Such considerations could have figured in Channing Lewis's decision to move to Massachusetts. More likely, in keeping with a pattern common to migrants before and since, he chose his destination because of kinship ties. In Springfield he joined his brother, Edward Rudolph Lewis, who had settled in the city some years before. About seventeen years older than Channing, Edward had fled Virginia in 1864 and enlisted in the Ohio Volunteers of the U.S. Colored Infantry. After the war Edward had remained in the North, supported in part by a federal pension of $120 per year for his service in the Union Army.[2]

By the time Channing arrived, Edward was a well-established figure within Springfield's small but relatively stable black community. In the early 1880s that community consisted of some 700 individuals, about 2 percent of a total population of 35,000. Like the Lewises, many of the city's blacks had emigrated from the upper South—from Maryland, North Carolina, and South Carolina as well as Virginia. By 1914 southern blacks accounted for more than half of the nearly 1,800 black residents of Springfield, still little more than 2 percent of the city's population.[3]

Housing was not segregated in Springfield, and blacks lived in virtually every ward of the city except the most exclusive. Still, blacks met with discrimination and prejudice in their daily lives. "Oftentimes blacks were not waited on in stores," recalled one longtime resident, "and blacks were denied membership within white churches." Thus blacks tended to concentrate in two general areas: the "Hill" district in the southern end of the city and "downtown" to the north. Tenements and a few small businesses dominated the Hill, which was considered the more desirable of the two areas. Barber shops, furniture stores, and other black enterprises were located downtown, along with hotels and boardinghouses.[4]

Perhaps because he began as a peddler (or "convectioner," as his occupation is listed in the 1870 census), Edward Lewis took up residence in the commercially active downtown area of Springfield. Following his marriage to Mary A. Carter in 1872, he became a button maker, the job he held when his brother came to town, then a dealer in coal and wood. Later, either through an apprenticeship or by self-training, he became a stationary engineer, operating and maintaining steam engines, generators, and other machines. He is credited with inventing the "Lewis smoke device" for controlling the exhaust from steam engines. By 1897 Edward became sufficiently prosperous to purchase a house on Elm Street. Located downtown, this site was bought by the City of Springfield to create a park, now known as Court Square. He bought another house on Winthrop Street in 1904.[5]

Outside of work, Edward was an active participant in a wide range of African American organizations and institutions. He was one of twenty members of the elite black fraternity, the Sumner Lodge Post of the Masons, in which he served with distinction from 1880 to 1907. He also held membership in the E. K. Wilcox Post of the Grand Army, an affiliation of which he was especially proud.[6]

Fraternal organizations such as these figured importantly in the life of northern urban blacks. Reflecting a collective desire to create institutions that would provide the same social and

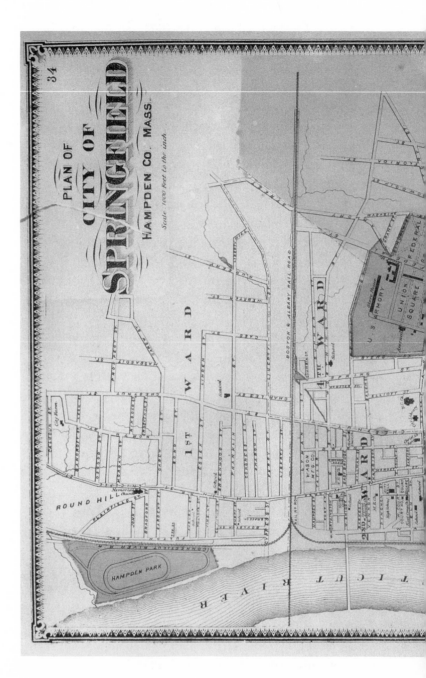

Map of Springfield, Massachusetts.
The darkened area at the center is the armory.
Channing Lewis lived on State Street at the armory's southern border.
The center of downtown lies directly to the left.
Main Street parallels the Connecticut River.
Courtesy of the Connecticut Valley Historical Museum.

economic advantages enjoyed by whites, they asserted a positive sense of racial identity. In addition to the Masonic and veterans groups to which Edward Lewis belonged, turn-of-the-century Springfield had black chapters of national organizations: the Harmony Lodge #140 of Elks and the Golden Chair Lodge #1549 of the Grand United Order of Odd Fellows. Similar groups for women included the Household of Ruth (an affiliate of the Odd Fellows), the Mary Garnet Club, the Elizabeth Carter and Abbie Shaw Club, the May Highland Garnet Club, and the [Mrs.] Francis Earl Wilson Club. Membership tended to be self-selective, attracting men and women who "had the interest of their race at heart." Although these organizations engaged in some political activity, they primarily served as centers of information, education, and mutual aid.[7]

By far the most vital institution in the "colored community," however, was the church. In Springfield three parishes shared that pivotal role: Loring Street African Methodist Episcopal, Third Baptist, and St. John's Congregational. By 1900 more than a thousand blacks belonged to one of these three churches. By 1914, of the 1,296 people designated as "colored" in Springfield, only 63—less than 5 percent—attended other churches with predominantly white congregations. Many of these were Roman Catholics who had recently emigrated from Portugal and the West Indies.[8]

The membership of the three churches reflected the composition of Springfield's black population at the time. Loring Street A.M.E. was the oldest, having been established in 1849 in the southern part of the city under the pastorship of Rev. George W. Bailey. Most of the church's members were migrants from the upper South and mid-Atlantic states who felt comfortable with the religious rituals and social structure of the African Methodist Episcopal faith. The congregation grew steadily over the years, from approximately 150 in the 1880s to more than 300 by 1914.

Whites in the surrounding community reacted negatively to the growth of the Loring Street church. In 1870, when the building was reconstructed as a chapel, whites living adjacent to the church property erected a high plank fence, which they painted black, on three sides. This glaring affront to the black parishioners of Loring Street A.M.E. remained until 1888, when Rev. T. R. Geda convinced the state legislature to pass an act requiring that the notorious "Black Fence" be removed.[9] Four years later, a new church building was erected on the site, and it still stands today.

The organization that came to be known as Third Baptist had its origins in 1869, when a group of blacks met at the homes of William M. Clark and Lucy Hicks on Hancock Street. In 1872 these families formed the Pilgrim Church; in 1876, a breakaway faction established the Berean Baptist Church. Five years later the Pilgrim and Berean congregations reunited as the Third Baptist Church. In the 1880s, Third Baptist experienced a rapid increase in membership, as the migration of blacks from the South gained momentum. Many southern blacks had been raised in the Baptist faith and Third Baptist offered the allure of the familiar. With a seating capacity of about 400 and a regular Sunday attendance of about 250, it soon became the largest of Springfield's black churches. Although located downtown, it drew its membership from throughout the city. This was the church that Edward Channing and his family joined and attended regularly. Edward was a leading figure there: he belonged to a select organization called the Van Horn Commandery of the Knights Templar, and family weddings and other activities were reported in The Church Bell, Third Baptist's newsletter.[10]

If Third Baptist could claim the most members, it was St. John's Congregational that was best known. Originally Zion's Methodist Episcopal Church, it began as a Methodist mission in 1849. In 1864 it became the Free Congregational Church; two years later it was renamed Sanford Street Congregational

"The colored chef" (Channing Lewis) as photographed
for "Progress on a New System," an article in the Springfield
Republican (3 May 1980) on the Little River
project. Courtesy of the Connecticut Valley Historical Museum.

Unidentified photograph found in *Alice Hanley's* letter
to Channing Lewis, 22 April 1906.

39 Carew Street, Springfield, Massachusetts, where
Alice Hanley Brennan lived in 1920.
Unidentified African American family in Springfield
ca. 1900. Courtesy of the Connecticut Valley Historical Museum.

Unidentified grade school children, Springfield, ca. 1900. Courtesy of the
Connecticut Valley Historical Museum.

Black-owned restaurant, Worthy Street, Springfield,
ca. 1900. Courtesy of the Connecticut Valley Historical Museum.
Below left, Third Baptist Church, 1910. Courtesy of the Connecticut
Valley Historical Museum. Below right, St. John's Church, 1901.
Courtesy of the Connecticut Valley Historical Museum.

Church. Eventually, the church took the name St. John's Congregational in honor of John Brown, the militant abolitionist, who had attended Zion Methodist when he lived in Springfield during the early 1850s.

Situated on the corner of Hancock and Union Streets in the Hill district, St. John's was the grandest of the black church structures when it was completed in 1911. As one black scholar observed a few years later, "St. John's Congregational Church has the distinction of possessing the most modern and the best equipped plant of the colored churches of New England."[11]

In many ways the black churches of late nineteenth-century Springfield embodied the decades-old tradition of community self-reliance, placing great importance on the establishment of viable and autonomous black institutions. In order to be independent, Loring Street A.M.E., Third Baptist, and St. John's all strove to be financially self-sufficient. St. John's, for example, relied on the support of its membership and followed the model of Fisk University's fabled Jubilee Singers, raising money through the efforts of its own singing group, the St. John's Double Quartet. Specializing in "the cultivation of southern plantation melodies and jubilee songs"—what came to be known as "Negro spirituals"—the Double Quartet helped spread the gospel while raising money for the church. In 1913 alone the group contributed more than $2000 to the church's building fund. While tax records from the early 1900s suggest that all three churches were relatively prosperous, the value of St. John's property holdings exceeded that of Loring Street A.M.E. and Third Baptist combined.

The churches also seemed to embrace Booker T. Washington's views concerning the value of "industrial education;" that is, educational training that could lead to gainful employment, and a social philosophy that placed moral uplift and community self-reliance above questions of civil and political rights. St. John's had a parish home and a home for "working girls," the latter completed in 1913 at a cost of $13,000 and designed "to offer to colored working girls and women the advantages and protection of a well-ordered Christian home." It also established a free employment bureau and a night school for training in the "domestic arts" in response to the urgent demand in New England for competent maids in household service. For the young men and women of the church, two social centers were constructed where they could read from "carefully selected books . . . local daily papers, the leading race journals, and a dozen or more good magazines." There was a club room for young men and boys, a basketball team, and a girls' club.[12]

The educational efforts of the churches complemented the instruction offered in the public schools. The *Springfield Graphic* commented in 1894 on the presence of "children having evidences of negro extraction" in the Pynchon Street kindergarten. In 1914, 286 blacks attended Springfield's grammar schools while sixteen were enrolled in the city's three high schools: Central High, Technical High, and the High School of Commerce. It is important to note that schooling was compulsory only to age fourteen. It is striking that of the six blacks who graduated from Central High School in 1913 and 1914, four went on to college. All attended segregated black colleges in the South: Tuskegee Institute, Morehouse and Spelman colleges, and Fisk University.[13]

The achievements of Springfield's black community rested upon a foundation of relative economic stability. Compared with blacks in other regions of the country, those in New England earned significantly higher wages. Historian William H. Harris has shown, for example, that by 1920 the per capita annual income of blacks in the Northeast was $436. By contrast, in the Midwest (Indiana, Illinois, Michigan, and Ohio), blacks earned $331 per year, while in the Pacific states the figure was $231.[14]

A 1914 survey of 894 black workers in Springfield found an

impressive number employed in a wide range of skilled and semi-skilled occupations. For black men, the traditional skilled trades were represented by teamsters (39), bricklayers (8), carpenters (7), painters (2), plumbers (2), printers (3), roofers (2), and tailors (6), among others. Other jobs requiring some skill or training included cooks (54), clerks (22), and machine operators (8). There was also a contingent of small-scale entrepreneurs, grocers (2), barbers (6), hostlers (7) as well as professionals, school teachers (5), clergymen (4), physicians (2), dentists (2). While the most common occupations for black women were domestic (186) and laundress (53), the survey also identified some skilled female workers, including dressmakers (16), nurses (10), and hairdressers (3).[15]

Upon closer scrutiny, however, the impression of widespread economic opportunity and upward social mobility proves somewhat misleading. If semi-skilled workers such as waiters, porters, elevator operators, and chauffeurs are grouped together with day laborers, jobbers, janitors, and domestic servants, then fully three-quarters (75.7 percent) of the black men and women surveyed could be classified as unskilled labor. Skilled workers compose only 22.4 percent of the total, and professionals less than 2 percent.

Although heavy industry formed the foundation of Springfield's economy by the 1880s, blacks were excluded from all but the most menial factory work. Similarly, municipal positions that offered economic mobility, stability, and status were denied to blacks; in 1914, only fifteen African Americans, mainly custodians, were employed by the city of Springfield. Federal jobs were even scarcer. In 1904 there was only one black postal clerk in Springfield and one mail carrier. This was nevertheless an improvement over the situation a decade earlier, when the only black postal worker was Austin T. Taylor, a custodian. A resident of the city since 1865, Taylor was appointed to his position in 1890, taking on the unofficial title of "Uncle Sam's Janitor." "There is no doubt existing in our minds," wrote Joseph Bowers in a 1914 study "The Springfield Negro," "that negroes are refused clerical employment because of their color."[16]

Almost all skilled trades required membership in unions, and most unions were totally closed to blacks. Only 69 of the 894 black workers surveyed in 1914 belonged to unions, most in the building trades or transportation. As one contemporary observer noted, it was "practically impossible" for African Americans to become stone masons, plasterers, or engineers, or to find work in the large textile mills because they could not obtain union membership. "Where the unions flourish," he continued, "colored men do not get employment." By contrast, Smith & Wesson Firearms hired more blacks than any other factory because it was a non-union shop.[17]

Racism was the core of the problem. Although de jure segregation was far more prevalent in the South, job discrimination against blacks was commonplace throughout the country. Despite the passage of the Fourteenth and Fifteenth Amendments, which guaranteed blacks equal protection under the law and secured the right of black men to vote, employers were free, in the unfettered and rapidly expanding industrial economy, to discriminate in hiring however they saw fit. And given the choice, most preferred to hire white workers rather than black workers, regardless of previous experience or qualification.

The huge influx of European immigrants during the last decades of the nineteenth century only made matters worse, adding to an already large pool of unskilled and semi-skilled labor and creating a downward pressure on wages for whites and blacks alike. The white and black working classes found themselves intermingling socially and building communities side by side; but they also found themselves inevitably forced into brutal competition for their narrowing share of the American pie. Such increased competition with newly arrived whites may help explain why Channing Lewis was never able to match the economic and social successes of his brother Edward, who came to Springfield in advance of the great waves of migration from the South and abroad.

After his arrival in Springfield, Channing first found work in a paper and cloth factory as a common laborer working for minimal wages. To make ends meet, he moved in with his brother, his sister-in-law Mary, and their three children, Mary, Florence, and Clarence, who ranged in age from two months to six years, in a multifamily tenement at 73 Stockbridge Street in the southern end of the city's downtown. Another brother, twenty-four-year-old John H. Lewis, his wife, Maggie, and their two children, George and Lydia, occupied a separate apartment at the same address. Extended family arrangements such as these were common among blacks and white European immigrants alike. In addition to pooling their resources to pay the rent, family members often shared responsibility for cooking, cleaning, child care, and other domestic chores.[18]

In less than a year, however, Channing left his brother's home, changing residences and jobs frequently between 1880 and 1882. He married Amelia Peters, a black woman born in the North, in 1882. Within two years they had a daughter, Grace, and a son named after Channing. Yet the promise of family and stability was short-lived. In 1884 both of the couple's young children died within a four-month period. Then, in August of the same year, Amelia herself also died, a victim of tuberculosis.[19]

We can only speculate as to how Channing Lewis managed to cope with this tragedy. Immeasurable as the emotional strain must have been, the financial burden of losing three members of his family so quickly would also have been enormous. Even the simplest funeral was costly, and with these expenses he might well have incurred the added debt of medical treatment. Although black fraternal organizations sometimes provided death benefits to members, there is no record that Channing Lewis, unlike his brother Edward, belonged to any of these groups. Nor is there any evidence that Channing was affiliated with any church, which would have been another possible source of financial support.

Whatever hardships he endured as a result of the death of his wife and children, Channing was still a young man at the time of his bereavement. Within a few years he established himself in a new line of work, as a cook. City directories list him as holding that position at five different restaurants during the 1880s and 1890s, including the restaurant at the train depot, the Belmont Hotel, and the Hayes House. Although the job lacked security, cooks could earn as much as fifty dollars a month, and as a result of the earning potential, the occupation ranked relatively high on the list of jobs available to blacks.[20]

In 1890 Channing remarried, this time to Josephine Murphy, a young Irish immigrant only three years in the United States. Her father was also a cook, and it is likely that Channing and Josephine met in the employment and social network of the restaurant trade. How the Lewis family responded to this second marriage is unknown. Interracial marriages, while not unheard of, were rare; in fact, Joseph Bowers's 1914 study cites just fifteen cases of marriage "between the races," eleven of them white women married to black men.[21] Such unions were as likely to be viewed with suspicion by blacks as by whites. African Americans were well aware that sexual relations between black men and white women—real or imagined, consensual or otherwise—supplied the rationale for much of the violence perpetrated against Southern blacks throughout the 1880s and 1890s. As publicized by Ida B. Wells and others, the incidence of lynchings escalated markedly during this period, and in most instances the pretext for these acts of mob murder was an alleged assault by a black man on a white woman. Even if interracial couples could count on a certain measure of tolerance outside the South, love across the color line still carried considerable risks.

One wonders, too, how Channing's relatives would have

regarded his marriage to a white woman. In black Springfield, single women outnumbered single men three to two, and the Lewises may well have questioned why Channing failed to marry one of their own.[22] Edward, with his stake in respectability and community leadership, might have been particularly affronted. Edward's active participation in a number of exclusively black organizations suggests a personal investment in the idea of an independent, if not wholly separate, black community. That Channing did not share his older brother's penchant for joining black self-help groups could indicate that the two brothers held fundamentally opposing views on issues of race. But it is also possible that their differences in this respect were at root temperamental or generational rather than philosophical.

Channing and Josephine took up residence at 46 East Williams Street in Springfield's Third Ward, seven blocks from his brother's house on Stockbridge Street and twelve blocks—or about three-quarters of a mile—from the restaurant where he worked on Vernon Street. In 1892 Josephine gave birth to the couple's only child, a daughter named after her mother. During the next few years Channing moved with his wife and child to two other locations on Williams Street. He also changed jobs, but without achieving any real upward mobility. In 1896 he took a job at Daniel and Kellogg's restaurant in Northampton, twenty miles north of Springfield along the Connecticut River. For the next two years he maintained residences in both cities, providing for his wife and daughter in Springfield while he himself lived at least part time in Northampton. He returned to Springfield in 1899 and when the census taker visited the Lewises the following year, she found a fairly typical working-class household: Channing was the chief breadwinner, but his wife brought in earnings washing clothes and looking after an African American lodger.[23]

It is possible that Channing first met Alice Hanley during his sojourn in Northampton. More likely, as Kathy Peiss suggests, their relationship developed after 1903, the year in which Channing separated from Josephine.

By August 1907, the date of the first extant letter from Alice to Channing, it is clear they were deeply involved with each other. In the letter, Alice announces her intention to stop by Channing's apartment in Springfield and pick up some belongings she had left there, and the letters that follow reveal that such visits were commonplace. Even though she lived in Northampton, the availability of cheap rail transport allowed her to shuttle frequently between the two cities. Once in Springfield, she could walk to Channing's apartment on State Street or take the trolley.

The evidence suggests that Alice and Channing never got together in Northampton, presumably to avoid the disapproving notice of Alice's family. In Springfield they could interact more openly. They could take walks, go shopping, eat at restaurants—do the kinds of things couples do that would have attracted more attention in the smaller city of Northampton. Whether their relationship was actually more accepted in Springfield is hard to know. As Ester Thompson, a longtime member of the Third Baptist Church, recalled, "Channing and Alice would have had a difficult time even within the black community."[24] Then again, it is possible that Alice was taken for a "high yellow gal," as light-skinned black women were then commonly known.

At the same time, Channing lived and worked in a mixed-race environment. Although his apartment was not far from the Hill, Channing's immediate neighborhood brought together lower-class blacks and whites, including a number of Italians and Irish Americans. His home was close to a number of middle-class residences, which often had live-in and day servants, and it was a short walk from downtown. The friends and neighbors who appear in Alice's letters were of different racial and ethnic backgrounds.[25] Perhaps in that heterogeneous milieu, an interracial couple would have been able to come and go without undue scrutiny.

In the absence of Channing's letters to Alice, it is impossible to know how he understood their relationship. Her letters to him nevertheless offer some clues. Aside from the expressions of endearment that Alice refers to, Channing seems to have genuinely cared for her. On one hand, he sent her money, not only to help defray some of her necessary expenses, from rail fare to eyeglasses, but also to fulfill her desire to be well dressed and respectable. On the other hand, Channing never divorced his second wife, who continued to live with their daughter in another part of town. He seems to have maintained some relationship with his daughter at least, until her premature death in 1909 at age seventeen. A charming photograph of a young light-complected black girl, with "Channing Lewis" written on the back, was in the envelope of Alice's letter of 22 April 1908; this was probably Channing's daughter. Channing never married Alice, despite her signing of two of the letters "your wife" and "your heartbroken wife." The letters also suggest that the relationship was plagued by escalating suspicion, and perhaps occasional violence.

Mistrust between the two lovers seems to have grown after Channing took a job that kept him away from his apartment for long stretches of time. In 1907 the city of Springfield launched a massive water filtration project centered at Little River Gorge. One phase of the contract was awarded to Charles Gow, a Boston-based civil engineer, who began construction on 1 May 1908, at Mundale, now part of Westfield. More than 400 men worked on the project, many of them recently arrived Italian immigrants recruited by contractor and saloon-keeper P. A. Breglio. Channing Lewis was hired as the cook for the engineers overseeing the project. "Their food is cooked and served by a colored chef," the *Springfield Republican* reported, "who is expert in the work."[26]

Expert or not, Lewis knew that this job, like others he had held over the years, would be temporary. Once the water project was completed, he would have to find work elsewhere. While he may have grown used to the chronically transitory nature of his work, it must have had a destabilizing effect on other aspects of his life, including his relationship with Alice. Reading Alice Hanley's letters, with their repeated pleas for Channing to deliver on his promises to send her money— money to pay for the outward appurtenances of a respectable life—one can imagine the tension her entreaties produced. No doubt he felt an unrelieved pressure to fulfill his assumed and expected role as a man by providing for Alice. Yet no matter how well Channing was paid for his expertise as a cook, he remained a black man in a society that afforded him little economic opportunity and even less financial security. Alice was not from the South and may not have fully understood the depth of the color line in America, nor the risks she was taking. Channing surely did.

Even if he found the circumstances of his own daily life to be tolerable—and we have no way of knowing if this was the case—Channing Lewis could not escape constant reminders of the inequities and injustices suffered by blacks in early twentieth-century America. We know he read the newspaper. Alice mentions seeing the Union, a Springfield daily, outside the door to Channing's apartment. During this period the Union and Springfield Republican, the leading daily newspapers, contained numerous stories of race riots, lynchings, and growing segregation throughout the country. In early 1908, for example, the Republican featured articles on efforts of the governor of Maryland to eliminate blacks from the voting rolls and on calls by Booker T. Washington for a total separation of the races, as well as one entitled, "First Lynching of the Year." Overall, the message that emerged from contemporary newspaper accounts was that slavery had been a benign institution, that the passage of the Fourteenth and Fifteenth Amendments had been a mistake, and that the South should be free to deal with its "Negro problem" without northern interference.[27]

These newspapers offered no discussion of political activity by blacks at either the national or the local level to meet the challenge of racism. In Springfield, such activity reached its height with the formation of the Negro Civil League in 1910, a year after the creation of the NAACP in New York. The two primary goals of the League were "the protection of our rights as citizens, and . . . the advancement of our political rights." In pursuit of these aims the League sponsored a series of lectures by prominent members of the African American community, including Mary McLeod Bethune and Rev. William N. De Berry of Springfield's St. John's Church. The League also encouraged blacks to maximize their political influence by pooling their votes, an effort that seems to have succeeded. As Joseph Bowers noted in his 1914 study, "The movement [led by the League] has completely solidified the negro vote."[28]

Yet the growing political unity of Springfield's black population could do little to reverse the trend toward increased racial polarization in the years that followed. Throughout the United States, lynchings and other brutalities against blacks became ever more common, culminating in the "Red Summer of 1919," when major race riots erupted in Omaha, Knoxville, Washington, and Chicago. The growing popularity of the Ku Klux Klan during the 1920s, in the North as well as the South, further testified to the worsening of American race relations.

These racial politics made it all the more difficult for men like Channing Lewis to love or marry white women, even when the circumstances of working-class life brought them together. Very little is known about Channing after his relationship with Alice ended. Edward Lewis died in 1912 and his family seemed to break apart after that: his son Clarence died in 1914, his wife and daughter went to Canada and later to Boston. Channing stayed in Springfield until 1918. He was not listed in the 1920 federal census of Massachusetts, but he returned to Springfield in 1922, again working as a cook. Between 1928 and 1934, his whereabouts are unknown, but then he reappears in Boston, where he lived until his death in 1941. His death certificate identifies him as the widower of

Josephine Murphy.[29] An old man of seventy-eight, Channing had experienced a lifetime of limited opportunities and personal tragedies, as had so many blacks in the racially segregated, industrializing United States. What it meant to Channing to seek love and companionship across the color line, not once but twice, remains a mystery. That he shared a dream of security, dignity, and home with Alice Hanley—and that the odds were against them—there can be little doubt.

## NOTES

1   Public records report Channing Lewis's date of birth variously from 1861 to 1866, although several records settle upon 1862 or 1863. See: U.S. Bureau of the Census, *Tenth Census of the United States,* 1880, *Population Schedules,* Springfield, Massachusetts; Marriage record, Channing M. Lewis and Josephine Murphy, 27 May 1890, 509, Springfield City Clerk's Office; *Twelfth Census of the United States,* 1900, *Population Schedules,* Springfield, Massachusetts, Enumeration District 589, sheet 7; Death certificate, no. 1214, Boston, 24 January 1941, Commonwealth of Massachusetts, State Department of Public Health, Registry of Vital Records and Statistics. On black migration, see Carter G. Woodson, *A Century of Negro Migration* (1918; reprint, New York: AMS Press, 1969); Robert Austin Warner, *New Haven Negroes: A Social History* (New Haven: Yale University Press, 1940); John Daniels, *In Freedom's Birthplace: A History of the Boston Negro* (1914; reprint, New York: Negro Universities Press, 1968); William Harris, *The Harder We Run: Black Workers Since the Civil War* (New York: Oxford University Press, 1981).

2   U.S. Bureau of the Census, *Eleventh Census of the United States,* 1890, *Special Schedule:* Surviving Soldiers, Sailors, and Marines . . . who served in the Army, Navy . . . during the War of the Rebellion, . . . in Springfield, County of Hampden, Massachusetts. Edward Lewis obituary, *Springfield Republican,* 27 April 1912.

3   Massachusetts Bureau of Labor Statistics, *Census of Massachusetts,* 1885 (Boston: Wright and Potter, 1887), vol. 1, pt. 1, 193; Massachusetts Bureau of Labor Statistics, *Census of the Commonwealth of Massachusetts,* 1895 (Boston: Wright and Potter, 1896), 1: 805–15; Massachusetts Bureau of Labor Statistics, *Decennial Census,* 1915 (Boston, 1918), 296, 314–23. Joseph William Bowers, "The Springfield Negro" (M.A. thesis, Springfield College, 1914); Joseph P. Lynch, "Blacks in Springfield, 1868–1880: A Mobility Study," *Historical Journal of Western Massachusetts* 7 (June 1979): 25–34.

4 Interviews with Ester Thompson, 8 July 1993 and Lovinia Stutts, 8 July 1993 (quotation from Thompson); Bowers, "Springfield Negro." On racial discrimination in New England, see John Hope Franklin, *From Slavery to Freedom*, 7th ed. (New York: Knopf, 1994), 277–322; Thomas J. Woofter, *Negro Problems in Cities* (Garden City, N.Y.: Doubleday, Doran, 1928); Woodson, *Century of Negro Migration*; Elizabeth Pleck, *Black Migration and Poverty, Boston, 1865–1900* (New York: Academic Press, 1979); Leonard Levy and Douglas L. Jones, *Jim Crow in Boston: The Origin of the Separate But Equal Doctrine* (New York: Da Capo Press, 1974); Lynch, "Blacks in Springfield."

5 U.S. Bureau of the Census, *Ninth Census of the United States, 1870, Population Schedules*, Springfield, Massachusetts, 86; *Tenth Census, 1880, Population Schedules*, Springfield; Edward R. Lewis, 60 Elm St., Springfield, Springfield City Clerk's Office, Registry of Deeds, 1897, book 554, 587; 1903, book 664, 33; 1904, book 686, 365. Edward R. Lewis, Probate Inventory, 21 November 1913, Commonwealth of Massachusetts, Hampden County Registry of Probate. *Springfield Directory* for the years from 1880 to 1895 (Springfield: Price and Lee, 1880–1895). Lewis obituary, *Springfield Republican*.

6 Moses King, ed., *King's Handbook of Springfield* (Springfield: James D. Gill, 1884), 218; *Springfield Directory*, 1905, 760.

7 Elmer Thompson, "A Study of the Negro of Springfield," manuscript, Springfield Technical College, 1904, 8–9, 13–15; Bowers, "Springfield Negro," 65–72.

8 On the black churches in Springfield, see Thompson, "Study of the Negro," 10–12; Bowers, "Springfield Negro," 43–64; King, *King's Handbook*, 190–91, 199–200, 203–4, 208, 219; Curtis Pierces Donnell, *Springfield Churches: 1636–1936* (Springfield: Springfield Republican, 1936), 23–25, 34–35, 38–39.

9 Donnell, *Springfield Churches*, 34.

10 Third Baptist Church, *The Church Bell* 1, no. 3 (November 1905), mentions Edward R. Lewis as a member of the standing committee and parish contributor; Channing's niece, Florence Lewis, as treasurer of the Ever Ready Committee; and the marriage of Channing's nephew, Clarence Lewis. In possession of Dorothy Jordan Pryor.

11 Bowers, "Springfield Negro," 47.

12 Ibid., 50, 56.

13 *Springfield Graphic*, 27 September 1894; Bowers, "Springfield Negro," 39–42; interview with Dorothy Jordan Pryor. Between 1905 and 1914, fifteen blacks graduated from Central High School: one in 1905, four in 1906, one in 1907, one in 1909, one in 1911, one in 1912, five in 1913, and one in 1914.

14　Harris, *Harder We Run*, 58; Bowers, "Springfield Negro," 19, 35–38.

15　Bowers, "Springfield Negro," 17–18; cf. Stephen Thernstrom, *The Other Bostonians: Poverty and Progress in the American Metropolis, 1880–1970* (Cambridge: Harvard University Press, 1973), 187, 194.

16　*Springfield Graphic*, 27 September 1894; Bowers, "Springfield Negro," 20.

17　Thompson, "Study of the Negro," 3–6; Bowers, "Springfield Negro," 18–19. On discrimination against blacks by unions, see F. E. Wolfe, *Admission to American Trade Unions* (Baltimore: Johns Hopkins University Press, 1912), chap. 6; W.E.B. Du Bois, *The Negro Artisan* (Atlanta: Atlanta University Press, 1902), 171; Paul Worthman, "A Black Worker and the Bricklayer's and Mason's Union, 1903," *Journal of Negro History* 54 (October 1969): 398–404; Horace R. Cayton and George S. Mitchell, *Black Workers and the New Unions* (Chapel Hill: University of North Carolina Press, 1939).

18　*Tenth Census, 1880, Population Schedules*, Springfield; *Springfield Directory*, 1880–1882.

19　*Springfield Directory* for the years from 1880–81 to 1886–87. Record of birth of Grace C. Lewis, 6 November 1882; Record of birth of Channing M. Lewis, 4 March 1884; Record of death of Amelia Peters Lewis, 11 August 1884, Book 1884, 71, all in Springfield City Clerk's Office.

20　*Springfield Directory* for the years 1886–87, 1891–92, 1895–96, 1899–1900, 1900–1901.

21　Marriage record, 27 May 1890; *Twelfth Census, 1900, Population Schedules*, Springfield, Enumeration District 589, sheet 7; Bowers, "Springfield Negro," 13–14.

22　Bowers, "Springfield Negro," 10, 12.

23　*Springfield Directory* for the years, 1891 to 1899. *Twelfth Census, 1900, Population Schedules*, Springfield.

24　Thompson interview.

25　U.S. Bureau of the Census, *Thirteenth Census of the United States, 1910, Population Schedules*, Springfield, Massachusetts Enumeration District 620, sheet 3.

26　"Progress on New System," *Springfield Republican*, 3 May 1908; *Little River: A Complete History and Pictorial Description of Superior Springfield's Superb New Water System* (Springfield: James F. McPhee, 1910).

27　See, for instance, *Springfield Republican* 3 January 1908, 18 January 1908.

28　Bowers, "Springfield Negro," 72–74.

29　*Springfield Directory* for the years from 1912 to 1917, 1922; *Boston City Directory* for the years from 1934–35 to 1939–40; Channing Lewis death certificate.